THE CONSCIENCE OF A CONSERVATIVE

YOUNG AMERICA'S FOUNDATION

Young America's Foundation is a tax exempt, non-partisan, educational organization dedicated to promoting the principles of free enterprise, individual liberty, and a strong national defense among American students. The Foundation performs this role with five basic programs. These include:

1. An annual summer conference in Washington for student leaders.
2. A national speakers program to promote a full and balanced public policy debate on our college campuses.
3. Scholarships for students who combine leadership with academic excellence.
4. Books and monographs on public policy, economics, history, and political thought.
5. Monitoring of the status of free speech on the college campuses.

The Foundation is classified by the Internal Revenue Service as a 501(c)(3) organization and as a "non private" (i.e., "public") foundation under section 509(a)(2). Contributions are tax exempt.

For information and literature, write or call:

Young America's Foundation
Suite 808
11800 Sunrise Valley Drive
Reston, Virginia 22091
Ph: 703/620-5270

THE CONSCIENCE OF A CONSERVATIVE

by

Barry Goldwater

with a New Introduction by
Patrick J. Buchanan

REGNERY GATEWAY
Washington, D.C.

Young America's Foundation
30th Anniversary Edition

Library of Congress Cataloging-in-Publication Data

Goldwater, Barry M. (Barry Morris), 1909–
  The conscience of a conservative / Barry Goldwater : with a new introduction by Patrick J. Buchanan.
      p. cm.
  Originally published: Shepherdsville, Ky. : Victor Pub. Co., 1960.
  ISBN 0-89526-540-0 (alk. paper). — ISBN 0-89526-754-3 (pbk. : alk. paper)
    1. United States—Politics and government—20th century.
  2. Conservatism—United States.   I. Title.
JK271.G668 1990
320.5'2'0973—dc20   89-78149
                                                              CIP

Published in the United States by
Regnery Gateway
1130 17th Street, NW
Washington, DC 20036

Manufactured in the United States of America.
10 9 8 7 6 5 4 3 2 1

TABLE OF CONTENTS

INTRODUCTION

The Voice in the Desert

by Patrick J. Buchanan

It was the final year of the Eisenhower Presidency.

The conservative young of the Silent Generation had joyously supported Ike in two campaigns against Adlai Stevenson, the champagne toast of the faculty lounge. But something was missing.

In 1956, the Hungarians, crying out for American help, had been abandoned, left to die under the treads of Soviet tanks. All of John Foster Dulles' talk of "rollback" had proven to be bluster and bluff. As the bloody tragedy played itself out on the streets of Budapest, America watched, waited, and did nothing. For days it went on. We were all sickened; and the sense of frustration and failure was all the greater because Moscow had taken the risk of war, and Moscow had won. And we all knew it.

The following year, Soviet rocket forces launched Sputnik. Moscow crowed, and anti-Americans all over the world celebrated. One month later, Vanguard, carrying the tiny three-pound answer of the United States, got four feet off the ground. Film of the fireball was shown in every theater in America. Though we laughed cynically, we felt humiliated. The "Russians," considered an ethnic joke, had made fools out of the United States.

America seemed on a downhill slide. Vice President Nixon was greeted by an angry mob in Caracas in 1958, and the recession-bitten Republican Party was routed, losing 12 Senate seats and 48 in the House.

January 1, 1959, Fidel Castro led his bearded columns into Havana, and defiantly began building a Communist state, 90 miles off the Florida coast. The American Left began an endless stream of pilgrimages to celebrate the brave new world rising in Havana. In October, Khrushchev came to tour; and some of us stood across the street from the White House in Lafayette Park, maintaining a stony silence as the "Butcher of Budapest" rolled by, waving and grinning, welcomed, here, in the Land of the Free, fêted at the White House by Ike himself. *Realpolitik* was in. Before Ike's return visit, a U-2 spy plane, flown by Francis Gary Powers, was shot down over Sverdlovsk. Khrushchev exploited the incident to dynamite the Paris summit and berate the American President.

In September, he showed up at the United Nations, every East European party boss and Fidel Castro in tow, pounding his fist and hammering his shoe on the tables of the General Assembly.

By 1960, with world war a receding memory and affluence accepted as a permanent condition, America's young were in search of a "cause" beyond themselves to which to dedicate their lives. "A man must share the action and passion of his time, at peril of being judged not to have lived," Justice Holmes had written. Because ours was the fortunate generation, the first truly free to determine its own destiny, many of us took the words to heart.

Forty-three-year-old Senator John F. Kennedy was capturing America's mood with his campaign cry of, "Let's get this country moving again!" Across the South, black students were conducting sit-ins, supported by white liberals of the Freedom Rides. Civil Rights had become the great cause of a liberalism on the move.

But what about the Right?

Into that winter of our discontent came this slim book. The effect was electric; thirty years later, the Senator would recall it:

The Conscience of a Conservative was the college student underground book of the times. It was virtually ignored by the media, most college professors, and other liberals, who had long held a monopoly on the information flowing to the American people. That first printing was ten thousand copies at three dollars each. Eventually, more than 4 million hardcover and paperback copies were sold . . . it became a rallying cry of the right against three decades of Franklin D. Roosevelt and the liberal agenda.

I was one of those students. When Barry Goldwater strode to the podium of Nixon's convention, to stop a spontaneous rally to put his name in nomination, roaring: "Let's grow up, conservatives, let's . . . take this party back—and I think we can someday. Let's go to work," I enlisted.

The Conscience of a Conservative was our new testament; it contained the core beliefs of our political faith, it told us why we had failed, what we must do. We read it, memorized it, quoted it. To re-read it today is to recall the magic the charismatic man from the desert had for so many thousands in that Silent Generation.

Every great movement—social, political, or religious—in its infancy, is marked by militancy. Its faithful shine with a spirit of sacrifice, a willingness to accept defeat and humiliation rather than compromise principal. Its True Believers are impatient, to the point of intolerance, with the half-hearted and the half-committed. He who is not with us is against us. That is the way we were.

And that is the temper of the bugle call to battle.

Like the man who produced it, the prose remains unembellished, simple, honest, straight, true. For those of us wandering in the arid desert of Eisenhower Republicanism, it hit like a rifle shot.

With its publication, Barry Goldwater became our champion; as his campaign would become the great cause of our youth. Though 1964 would end with media mockery of *The Party That Lost Its Head*, no winter would abate that spring's increase. The young conservatives, bonded and blooded in the Lost Cause of '64, would one day change the world.

After Mr. Nixon's narrow defeat, we knew in our hearts what the press did not dimly suspect. The Grand Old Party was ripe for the taking. So, too, was the golden boy of the Eastern Establishment, John F. Kennedy. In Barry Goldwater—that tanned, square-jawed, ex-army air corps pilot with the horn-rim glasses, straight talk, and sardonic humor—we had our candidate.

Like every smug establishment, the GOP was deaf to the sound of the trudging feet of the coming revolution. Relying, as ever, on money and media power, it could not match the fervor of those who fought for the true faith. As the Goldwater irregulars began to surface in state after state, the Establishment reassured itself that, surely, Nelson Rockefeller, landslide winner in New York, possessor of one of America's great fortunes, popular and progressive, could not be stopped. As the Establishment dozed in anticipation of its dream race between Rockefeller and JFK, we were at work.

A twenty-three-year-old graduate student at Columbia, a right-wing oddity in the premier journalism school in the country, I was a Goldwater zealot. In 1962, I led a delegation of amused and skeptical fellow students down to Madison Square Garden for the giant rally held by the Young Americans for Freedom, featuring the leaders of the movement, with Goldwater speaking last. It was the beginning of the 1960s. Outside, a huge crowd of shouting, cursing leftists had to be held back by mounted police. Crewcut versus longhair, we traded angry insults as we entered the hall. After the rally, I went over to YAF headquarters to volunteer to write press releases at night to advance the cause; and made a futile application to *National Review*, William F. Buckley's brilliant magazine that was the spark of the revolution.

Like a first love, the Goldwater campaign was, for thousands of men and women now well into middle age, an experience that will never recede from memory, one on which we look back with pride and fond remembrance. We were there on St. Crispin's Day. I have never met an old "Goldwaterite" who thought that perhaps we should have gone with Rockefeller, Scranton, or Lodge. Because the cause appeared hopeless, because the crew-cut militants of the Goldwater movement were relentlessly demonized as racist and reactionary, there were few trimmers and time-servers in the all-volunteer Goldwater army. In those days, at least, the phrase "conservative opportunist" was a contradiction in terms.

All of us of that generation remember where we were Black Friday, November 22, 1963, when the bulletin came over the ticker that John F. Kennedy had been shot in Dallas. That morning, I was polishing a 1500-word op-ed piece for the St. Louis Globe-Democrat, where I was writing editorials, predicting our movement would carry Goldwater to the nomination, and beyond. Now that JFK has been enshrined in memory by that awful act, and by those indelible days after Dallas, it has been forgotten how ineffectual, how vulnerable, he seemed in the fall of 1963.

With the squalid murder of President Diem and his brother in Saigon in early November, with U.S. complicity in the palace coup being investigated, with JFK checkmated on the Hill, with rising press resentment of his "news management" and use of wiretaps on the steel industry, with civil rights leaders openly challenging his commitment, the country was picking up on the slogan, "Less Profile, More Courage." Victor Lasky's scathing biography, *JFK, the Man and the Myth*, was a best seller, being serialized in newspapers all over America. The President was in deep trouble. Indeed, that was why he was down in Texas, trying to mend broken fences that could have cost him the state in 1964.

Because the American Right, by November 1963, was the most visible and visceral adversary of JFK, we bore the onus of the recriminations. It may not have been a "right-wing nut" who pulled the trigger, the argument ran, but the Right "created the climate." I yet remember the stares of cold hatred from those with whom we had argued passionately over the merits of JFK. The bullet that took President Kennedy's life mortally wounded the Goldwater movement as well.

Suddenly, politics, which had seemed so full of promise, was poisoned at the well. In his memoir, Goldwater writes that all his hope for a gentleman's contest with Jack Kennedy, his old friend and antagonist from the Senate, vanished with the arrival of Lyndon Baines Johnson and the politics of "paranoia and cold deceit."

Rarely has an American patriot been subjected to so savage a campaign.

An enemy of discrimination all his life, Goldwater argued that faithfulness to the Constitution was more important than even the most salutary reform that might come of restricting the freedoms the Constitution guaranteed. Discrimination is wrong, he said, but it is not the business of the Federal Government to supplant state government, or to dictate the private conduct of free, if misguided, men. With a small handful, he bravely stood up and cast a futile "no" vote on the Civil Rights Act of 1964.

And the vilification began.

Walter Lippmann denounced him as a "demagogue who dreams of arousing the rich against the poor," a man who would convert the Party of Lincoln into "a White man's party," a reactionary, "who would dissolve the Federal union into a mere confederation of the states . . . [and] nullify if he could the central purpose of the Civil War amendments and . . . take from the children of the emancipated slaves the protection of the national union."

This, about a candidate who went down to the White House to ask LBJ to agree to a moratorium on any discussion of "race" in the campaign, lest the nation be further divided. Compared to the others, Lippmann, dean of American journalists, was magnanimous.

In "Thunder on the Right," CBS linked Goldwater to the most extreme elements in America; Daniel Schorr flew to Bavaria to suggest the GOP nominee was coming to "Hitler's onetime stomping ground" to link up with neo-Nazis. "There are signs," Schorr said, "that the American and German right wings are joining up."

"[T]he most irresponsible reporting I've witnessed in my life," the Senator said, but the damage was done.

The first television attack ads appeared, handiwork of LBJ's Artful Dodger, Bill Moyers. One showed two hands tearing apart a Social Security card. Another, the "Daisy Girl" ad, had a little girl picking flowers as an ominous voice counted down to zero—to a nuclear explosion and fireball in which she disappeared. Then, a voice: "These are the stakes: To make a world in which all of God's children can live, or go into the dark. We must either love each other or we must die. Vote for President Johnson on November third. The stakes are too high for you to stay at home."

"Electronic dirt," the Senator called it; but it was effective. Conservatives in 1964 were utterly unprepared for the savagery of the no-holds-barred campaign conducted by the Left. After their baptism of fire and crushing defeat, they would go back and study the new rules of political warfare, and the Left, which invented modern attack politics would one day cry "foul," when their own captured weapons were turned against them.

While the Goldwater campaign was scarcely an unflawed enterprise, the portrayal of Mr. Conservative as war-monger, racist, and enthusiast of fascism was a lie, a Big Lie that convinced millions of young conservatives that the press' claim to objectivity and neutrality in national politics was a textbook case of consumer fraud. In the campaign of '64, conservatives acquired a distrust of the media that yet endures.

Ensconced in the "ivory tower" of an editorial page, I watched in frustration as the Senator's campaign mistakes were exploited by the Democrats, aided by a collaborationist press which converted this patriot into a sordid caricature of a man of the Right: ignorant, cold-hearted, racist, unreflective, militaristic.

The moment came for my paper, *The St. Louis Globe*, to endorse a candidate. The publisher—at the directive of the paper's owner, S. I. Newhouse, a friend of LBJ—refused to endorse either candidate. Our endorsement of Goldwater would have made no difference; its absence was a national news story, a shattering blow to campaign morale. It was not only the 300,000 readers of *The Globe* in the bi-state area who were stunned; the paper was then among the most stalwart conservative voices in America. What we were saying to Missouri, Illinois, and America was that Senator Barry Goldwater, whom we had championed for years, did not merit solid support in November. Conservatives could, in good conscience, take a walk, or vote for LBJ.

As the publisher flew off to Chicago, I took the phone calls from the bitter, the enraged, the broken-hearted. For days they came. Inescapable was the sense that we were behaving like the other turncoats, the Rockefeller, Javits crowd, all of us lacking the moral courage to go down to defeat with a man who had won the nomination fair and square. We had bailed out; we had cut and run. Observing the one-sided brawl from the press box, I made a promise: Next time, I would be down on the field.

Senator Goldwater was crushed, politically and personally; he would never again consider national office. But his defeat, like the receding of the Nile, left layers of fertile soil on the banks of our national politics.

Conservatives had captured the party; they had done it with ideas; they had recruited a national movement; they had battle-tested thousands of young men and women who would play larger roles in coming decades. And 1964 had begun the political career of a transplanted Texan, George Bush, who headed up the Harris County committee for Barry Goldwater; and it launched a second career for a faltering actor named Ronald Reagan.

Stunning in its breadth and depth, the Goldwater defeat drove the conservative movement back to the catacombs; the news media wrote us off and laughed us off.

The GOP was left with but two visible national leaders.

The first was George Romney, who had put distance between himself and Goldwater; the second was Richard Nixon, who had campaigned for the Goldwater-Miller ticket as hard as the nominee himself. I decided Nixon was the man. So, too, had Mr. Conservative. In January 1965, he told Nixon privately that if Dick Nixon ever needed Barry Goldwater for another run at the GOP nomination, he would be there. By December 1965, I, too, was there, having signed on with Richard Nixon after an arranged midnight meeting in the kitchen of premier conservative cartoonist, Don Hesse, in Belleville, Illinois.

The former Vice President had set his sights on a great GOP comeback in 1966, but he was also looking over the horizon. The most acute mind in American politics needed no tutoring to read the new balance of power in the GOP.

In 1960, Nixon had traveled to New York to sign the Treaty of Fifth Avenue with Nelson Rockefeller; by 1965, the old establishment that Rockefeller represented was dethroned, and the revolution was in power.

Moving quickly, but quietly in 1966 and 1967, the former Vice President began to line up Senators Goldwater, Tower, and Thurmond, and to win the support of columnists William F. Buckley, Jr., James J. Kilpatrick, John Chamberlain, and a dozen others. Before Ronald Reagan ever appeared on the radar screen of national politics, Nixon had already assembled his armada of conservative support.

But, as Nixon moved inexorably toward the Republican nomination for the presidency of the United States, a sea change had taken place in American politics.

In 1960, the difference between liberals and conservatives, Democrats and Republicans, was narrower than today. Indeed, so close were JFK and Nixon in their campaign promises that Arthur Schlesinger felt compelled to produce a campaign book, pointing up the differences. In the 1950s, Americans agreed about what the Good Society was; we disagreed over how to reach it. We knew who our enemy was; we disagreed over how to wage the Cold War.

Senator Goldwater, to the right of Nixon, was a Robert Taft conservative. He sought a retreat of federal power from duties that belonged to states, cities, communities, and citizens; he wanted an end to federal interference in agriculture, housing, education, and civil rights. But in fighting the Cold War, he wanted the United States to go onto the offensive, to end the struggle between Communism and the West in a victory for freedom.

These were the battle lines of 1960; in this book, they are drawn clearly and sharply. But, in the crucial decade that followed, a schism of the soul opened in America. Suddenly, the battle lines of politics were extended through the culture. Suddenly, we not only disagreed about how to wage Cold War, but about whether America was a good country serving a moral purpose in the world.

As we marched deeper and deeper into Vietnam, a militant

New Left gathered strength, declared traditional patriotism to be disloyalty to a higher ideal, and attempted a takeover of the Party of Truman, LBJ, and JFK. Not only was our involvement unwise, they said, we were fighting a dirty, immoral war. Suddenly, in peace demonstrations, there appeared the Viet Cong flags of an enemy that was then ambushing and killing U.S. troops.

The civil rights movement, too, had changed. While it had won the nation's allegiance to the ideal of equal opportunity and equal rights, suddenly it had a new agenda: Black Power and equality of result, a socialist ideal.

Compulsory integration of the public schools must be brought about by court-ordered busing if necessary, black leaders insisted; there must be full integration of neighborhoods, through the use of subsidized housing. Desegregation is no longer enough. Blacks are entitled not only to equal opportunity, but an equal share of jobs. If quotas must be used in hiring and promotion, and racial set-asides in government contracts, so be it. Americans who had united on the old agenda of civil rights parted company once again.

By 1968, the Supreme Court, led by Chief Justice Warren, had unleashed a social revolution, striking down state laws against pornography, tilting the legal system toward criminal defendants, ordering prayer and the Bible out of public education, and, one day soon, converting abortion, a universal crime in the 1950s, into a newly invented constitutional right.

The depth of the division was everywhere visible. I yet recall taking off on a night flight from La Guardia to Logan, with Richard Nixon, February 1, 1968, to enter New Hampshire's primary, as word came of a surprise Tet offensive across South Vietnam. Before the primaries were over, LBJ, his presidency broken, had announced he would not run again; Martin Luther King, Jr., had been assassinated in Memphis; the worst riots in U.S. history had gutted 100 American cities; campus revolts closed down Columbia and a dozen colleges; Robert F. Kennedy had been murdered in Los Angeles. Sent by Richard Nixon to be his observer at the Democratic Convention in Chicago, I watched the party come apart in the street below, with Dick Daley's cops beating the demonstrators who had provoked them night after night. Meanwhile, other boys, by the hundreds, were coming home in body bags, to be buried in the small towns of Middle America.

America's division was reflected in a presidential election that left Republicans and Democrats each with 43 percent of the vote, with 10,000,000 voters bolting to George Wallace, segregationist Governor of Alabama.

Much of the national press had defected to the revolution, to the counter-culture, to the black militants, to the anti-war movement, as America's second civil war was fought out—inside the Democratic Party.

Ethnic Democrats—Irish, Poles, Italians, Balts—from northern cities, whom some of us in the Nixon campaign had courted for three years, were being herd-driven into our corral by demagogic assault from the radical Left. Catholics who had given Jack Kennedy 80 percent of their votes in 1960, and Southern whites who had remained loyal to Adlai Stevenson, were being branded "gun nuts," "racists," "rednecks," "Bubbas," "reactionaries," and "kooks," for not embracing the new agenda. We could not believe our luck. Called Social Conservatives, they came over, by the millions.

While economic conservatives who believed private enterprise was the locomotive of progress had always been Republican, anti-Communists and social conservatives had belonged to both parties. Harry Truman would have been no more comfortable with Gay Liberation than Spiro Agnew was; JFK and LBJ carried anti-Communist credentials that matched those of Eisenhower and Nixon.

The Emerging Republican Majority of Kevin Phillips' depiction, which swept 49 states in 1972, however, suddenly hit a reef called Watergate. With the resignations of Richard Nixon and Spiro Agnew, and the recession of 1974, the New Majority coalition was broken, and the conservative tide that was carrying the GOP to majority party status, broke, and, temporarily, receded.

In retrospect, the GOP's defeat in 1976 was among the most fortunate of events in the history of conservatism. With Mr. Carter's capture of the White House, with liberals, from 1977 to 1981, holding all seats of power, from Congress to the courts, from the bureaucracy to the media, the stage was set for the ideological showdown of 1980. Perfect casting came, with the GOP's decision to nominate the man who had succeeded Senator Goldwater as Mr. Conservative.

So it was that twenty years after this book appeared, Ronald Reagan took his oath, looking west as he delivered his inaugural address. Without the man who wrote *The Conscience of a Conservative*, and the movement it inspired, there would have been no Conservative Decade.

Looking back in 1990, the question needs answering: Did we keep the faith?

Following Goldwater's counsel, Ronald Reagan moved beyond containment to a Reagan Doctrine of rolling back the Communist Empire from its most vulnerable outposts in Grenada, Nicaragua, Angola, Afghanistan. By 1990, Communism was in collapse in Eastern Europe and in retreat around the world. Conservatism triumphed.

Guided by senior adviser and later Attorney General Ed Meese, President Reagan began the recapture of the federal courts for constitutionalism. By 1990, with his vice president now his successor in the White House—there in part because Barry Goldwater had gone to New Hampshire in George Bush's hour of need, to endorse his old Harris County chairman—the day seemed not too distant, when, with the departure of octogenerian justices Brennan, Blackmun, and Marshall, a Rehnquist-Scalia Supreme Court would become reality.

In tax policy, Ronald Reagan did not take the nation all the way to a flat tax, which Barry Goldwater had urged, but he took us further than critics thought possible, rolling back federal income tax rates from 70 to 28 percent, igniting the longest peacetime expansion in U.S. history.

We failed utterly, however, to check the growth of government.

Federal spending yet consumes more than one-fifth of the nation's Gross National Product, and, since Barry Goldwater wrote this book, the *federal government has created no fewer than five new cabinet departments:* Housing and Urban Development, Transportation, Energy, Education, and Veterans' Affairs.

"The Federal Government," the Senator had written, "has moved into every field in which it believes its services are needed. . . . The result is a Leviathan, a vast national authority out of touch with people, and out of their control. This monopoly of power is bounded only by the will of those who sit in high places." Leviathan survived the Reagan Revolution.

Where Senator Goldwater had castigated an Eisenhower-built Department of Health, Education and Welfare consuming $15 billion a year, the budget for its successor agency, the Department of Health and Human Services, is now $300 billion; and the nation's debt approaches $3 trillion.

Among the "great evils of Welfarism is that it transforms the individual from a dignified, industrious, self-reliant *spiritual* being into a dependent animal creature without his knowing it," Goldwater wrote. "There is no avoiding this damage to character under the Welfare State." Perhaps 20 million Americans now occupy a federal plantation which has also survived the Reagan Revolution. And, black America, special target of LBJ's War on Poverty, now experiences levels of crime and violence, alcohol and drug abuse, teen pregnancy and suicide, destitution and despair, unimaginable in the 1950s. The altruists who launched the Great Society visited more social damage on black America than did segregation or the Depression.

Believing in Jefferson's "natural aristocracy," the Senator had special scorn for the social levelers: "Subscribing to the egalitarian notion that every child must have the same education, we have neglected to provide an educational system which will tax the talents and stir the ambitions of our best students and which will thus insure us the kind of leaders we will need in the future." What America's schools once did, Japan's schools now do.

In many ways, conservatives served America well, but we accepted truces in too many battles, we surrendered, outright, on too many fronts. Ours is, thus, an unfinished revolution.

And, during the conservative decade, the schism in America's soul deepened, manifesting itself in new conflicts.

We see it in violent disagreement on Central America, where revolutionary Marxists seek to impose their rule on 25 million people, and, one day, to bring their revolution home to the "belly of the beast."

We see it in the fading away of the Free Society—where men advanced on ability, merit, and performance—and the substitution of a spoils system where jobs and contracts are contingent on handicap, race, and sex.

We see it in a self-indulgent hedonism among the affluent and the young, that makes us wonder whether America is going the way of Rome, that raises the question of whether we are still a good country, as well as a great one. "Men have forgotten God," Solzhenitsyn wrote of his beloved Russian people; it is too true today of Americans. For that, government has no answer.

And the old challenges remain:

Forty-five years after Hitler perished in his bunker, we have 300,000 troops defending rich, prosperous Western Europe. Thirty years after Barry Goldwater told us to get out of the business of international welfare, we shovel out $15 billion in annual foreign aid to failed socialist and Marxist regimes. We still put the full faith and credit of our empty Treasury and our status as a debtor nation behind the bad loans of globalist bureaucrats.

In this sermon of fire and brimstone that is *The Conscience of a Conservative*, Barry Goldwater had the answers, if only we had followed his wise counsel.

"The turn will come," he had written, "when we entrust the conduct of our affairs to men who understand that their first duty as public officials is to divest themselves of the power they have been given. It will come when Americans . . . decide to put the man in office who is pledged to enforce the Constitution and restore the Republic. Who will proclaim in a campaign speech, 'I have little interest in streamlining government or in making it more efficient, for I mean to reduce its size. I do not undertake to promote welfare for I propose to extend freedom. My aim is not to pass laws, but to repeal them. It is not to inaugurate new programs but to cancel old ones that do violence to the Constitution.' " The marching orders of 1960 remain wise counsel for 1990.

Looking back, those of us who believed in Barry Goldwater have nothing to regret, and much to be proud of. We did indeed lose in a cause that would one day triumph. "Bliss was it in that dawn to be alive/But to be young was very heaven!" Wordsworth wrote of an earlier revolution; it was also true of ours.

What became of the other "causes" of the 1960s?

The civil rights movement would triumph, but, today, it has degenerated into a clamorous special interest demanding racial preference. The sexual revolution would gutter out in the epidemics of herpes and AIDS. The "peace" movement would give us Cambodia and the boat people. The feminists would enter the new decade championing the cause of unrestricted abortion and lesbian rights.

Written off as the Indian summer of Taft Republicanism, a politics of nostalgia, our movement proved the more enduring.

Twenty years after Barry Goldwater wrote this book, we took over the U.S. government, restored the nation's might and morale, gave her ten years of peace and prosperity unseen since the 1920s, and won the Cold War. Not bad, not bad at all. But, as Ronald Reagan used to say, the best is yet to come.

FOREWORD

T_{HIS} B_{OOK} is not written with the idea of adding to or improving on the Conservative philosophy. Or of "bringing it up to date." The ancient and tested truths that guided our Republic through its early days will do equally well for us. The challenge to Conservatives today is quite simply to demonstrate the bearing of a proven philosophy on the problems of our own time.

I should explain the considerations that led me to join in this effort. I am a politician, a United States Senator. As such, I have had an opportunity to learn somthing about the political instincts of the American people, I have crossed the length and breadth of this great land hundreds of times and talked with tens of thousands of people, with Democrats and Republicans, with farmers and laborers and businessmen. I find that America is fundamentally a Conservative nation. The preponderant judgment of the American people, especially of the young people, is that the radical, or Liberal, approach has not worked and is not working. They yearn for a return to Conservative principles.

At the same time, I have been in a position to observe first hand how Conservatism is faring in Washington. And it is all too clear that in spite of a Conservative revival among the people the radical ideas that were promoted by the New and Fair Deals under the guise of Liberalism still dominate the councils of our national government.

In a country where it is now generally understood and proclaimed that the people's welfare depends on individual self reliance rather than on state paternalism, Congress annually deliberates over whether the *increase* in government welfarism should be small or large.

In a country where it is now generally understood and proclaimed that the federal government spends too much, Congress annually deliberates over whether to raise the federal budget by a few billion dollars or by many billion.

In a country where it is now generally understood and proclaimed that individual liberty depends on decentralized government, Congress annually deliberates over whether vigorous or halting steps should be taken to bring state government into line with federal policy.

In a country where it is now generally understood and proclaimed that Communism is an enemy bound to destroy us, Congress annually deliberates over means of "co-existing" with the Soviet Union.

And so the question arises: Why have American people been unable to translate their views into appropriate political action? Why should the nation's underlying allegiance to Conservative principles have failed to produce corresponding deeds in Washington?

I do not blame my brethren in government, all of whom work hard and conscientiously at their jobs. I blame Conservatives—ourselves—myself. Our failure, as one Conservative writer has put it, is the failure of the Conservative demonstration. Though we Conservatives are deeply persuaded that our society is ailing, and know that Conservatism holds the key to national salvation—and feel sure the country agrees with us—we seem unable to demonstrate the practical relevance of Conservative principles to the needs of the day. We sit by impotently while Congress seeks to improvise solutions to problems that are not the real problems facing the country, while the government attempts to assuage imagined concerns and ignores the real concerns and real needs of the people.

Perhaps we suffer from an over-sensitivity to the judgments of those who rule the mass communications media. We are daily consigned by "enlightened" commentators to political oblivion: Conservatism, we are told, is out-of-date. The charge is preposterous and we ought boldly to say so. The laws of God, and of nature, have no dateline. The principles on which the Conservative political position is based have been established by a process that has nothing to do with the social, economic and political landscape that changes from decade to decade and from century to century. These principles are derived from the nature of man, and from the truths that God has revealed about His creation. Circumstances do change. So do the problems that are shaped by circumstances. But the principles that govern the solution of the problems do not. To suggest that the Conservative philosophy is out of date is akin to saying that the Golden Rule, or the Ten Commandments or Aristotle's *Politics* are out of date. The Conservative approach is nothing more or less than an attempt to apply the wisdom and experience and the revealed truths of the past to the problems of today. The challenge is not to find new or different truths, but to learn how to apply established truths to the problems of the contemporary world. My hope is that one more Conservative voice will be helpful in meeting this challenge.

This book is an attempt to bridge the gap between theory and practice. I shall draw upon my speeches, the radio and television broadcasts and the notes I have made over the years in the hope of doing what one is often unable to do in the course of a harried day's work on the Senate floor: to show the connection between Conservative principles so widely espoused, and Conservative action, so generally neglected.

THE
CONSCIENCE
OF A
CONSERVATIVE

CHAPTER ONE

The Conscience
of a Conservative

I HAVE BEEN much concerned that so many people today with Conservative instincts feel compelled to apologize for them. Or if not to apologize directly, to qualify their commitment in a way that amounts to breast-beating. "Republican candidates," Vice President Nixon has said, "should be economic conservatives, but conservatives with a heart." President Eisenhower announced during his first term, "I am conservative when it comes to economic problems but liberal when it comes to human problems." Still other Republican leaders have insisted on calling themselves "progressive" Conservatives.* These formulations are tantamount to an admission that Conservatism is a narrow, mechanistic *economic* theory that may work very well as a book-

---

*This is a strange label indeed: it implies that "ordinary" Conservatism is opposed to progress. Have we forgotten that America made its greatest progress when Conservative principles were honored and preserved.

keeper's guide, but cannot be relied upon as a comprehensive political philosophy.

The same judgment, though in the form of an attack rather than an admission, is advanced by the radical camp. "We liberals," they say, "are interested in *people*. Our concern is with human beings, while you Conservatives are preoccupied with the preservation of economic privilege and status." Take them a step further, and the Liberals will turn the accusations into a class argument: it is the little people that concern us, not the "malefactors of great wealth."

Such statements, from friend and foe alike, do great injustice to the Conservative point of view. Conservatism is *not* an economic theory, though it has economic implications. The shoe is precisely on the other foot: it is Socialism that subordinates all other considerations to man's material well-being. It is Conservatism that puts material things in their proper place—that has a structured view of the human being and of human society, in which economics plays only a subsidiary role.

The root difference between the Conservatives and the Liberals of today is that Conservatives take account of the *whole* man, while the Liberals tend to look only at the material side of man's nature. The Conservative believes that man is, in part, an economic, an animal creature; but that he is also a spiritual creature with spiritual needs and spiritual desires. What is more, these needs and desires reflect the *superior* side of man's nature, and thus take precedence over his economic wants. Conservatism therefore looks upon the enhancement of man's spiritual nature as the primary concern of political philosophy. Liberals, on the other hand, — in the name of a concern for "human beings" — regard the satisfaction of economic wants as the dominant mission of society. They are, moreover, in a hurry. So that their characteristic approach is to harness the society's political and economic forces into a collective effort to *compel* "progress." In this approach, I believe they fight against Nature.

Surely the first obligation of a political thinker is to understand the nature of man. The Conservative does not claim special powers of perception on this point, but he does claim a familiarity with the accumulated wisdom and experience of history, and he is not too proud to learn from the great minds of the past.

The first thing he has learned about man is that each member of the species is a unique creature. Man's most sacred possession is his individual soul — which has an immortal side, but also a mortal one. The mortal side establishes his absolute differentness from every other human being. *Only a philosophy that takes into account the essential differences between men, and, accordingly, makes provision for developing the different potentialities of each man can claim to be in accord with Nature.* We have heard much in our time about "the common man." It is a concept that pays little attention to the history of a nation that grew great through the initiative and ambition of uncommon men. The Conservative knows that to regard man as part of an undifferentiated mass is to consign him to ultimate slavery.

Secondly, the Conservative has learned that the economic and spiritual aspects of man's nature are inextricably intertwined. He cannot be economically free, or even economically efficient, if he is enslaved politically; conversely, man's political freedom is illusory if he is dependent for his economic needs on the State.

The Conservative realizes, thirdly, that man's development, in both its spiritual and material aspects, is not something that can be directed by outside forces. Every man, for his individual good and for the good of his society, is responsible for his *own* development. The choices that govern his life are choices that *he* must make: they cannot be made by any other human being, or by a collectivity of human beings. If the Conservative is less anxious than his Liberal brethren to increase Social Security "benefits," it is because he is more anxious than his Liberal brethren that people be free throughout their lives to spend their earnings when and as they see fit.

So it is that Conservatism, throughout history, has

regarded man neither as a potential pawn of other men, nor as a part of a general collectivity in which the sacredness and the separate identity of individual human beings are ignored. Throughout history, true Conservatism has been at war equally with autocrats and with "democratic" Jacobins. The true Conservative was sympathetic with the plight of the hapless peasant under the tyranny of the French monarchy. And he was equally revolted at the attempt to solve that problem by a mob tyranny that paraded under the banner of egalitarianism. The conscience of the Conservative is pricked by *anyone* who would debase the dignity of the individual human being. Today, therefore, he is at odds with dictators who rule by terror, and equally with those gentler collectivists who ask our permission to play God with the human race.

With this view of the nature of man, it is understandable that the Conservative looks upon politics as the art of achieving the maximum amount of freedom for individuals that is consistent with the maintenance of social order. The Conservative is the first to understand that the practice of freedom requires the establishment of order: it is impossible for one man to be free if another is able to deny him the exercise of his freedom. But the Conservative also recognizes that the political power on which order is based is a self-aggrandizing force; that its appetite grows with eating. He knows that the utmost vigilance and care are required to keep political power within its proper bounds.

In our day, order is pretty well taken care of. The delicate balance that ideally exists between freedom and order has long since tipped against freedom practically everywhere on earth. In some countries, freedom is altogether down and order holds absolute sway. In our country the trend is less far advanced, but it is well along and gathering momentum every day. Thus, for the American Conservative, there is no difficulty in identifying the day's overriding political challenge: it is *to preserve and extend freedom*. As he surveys the various attitudes and institutions and laws that currently prevail in America, many questions will occur to him, but the Conservative's first concern will always be: *Are we maximizing freedom?* I suggest we examine some of the critical issues facing us today with this question in mind.

CHAPTER TWO

The Perils of Power

T HE NEW DEAL, Dean Acheson wrote approvingly in a book called *A Democrat Looks At His Party*, "conceived of the federal government as the whole people organized to do what had to be done." A year later Mr. Larson wrote *A Republican Looks At His Party*, and made much the same claim in his book for Modern Republicans. The "underlying philosophy" of the New Republicanism, said Mr. Larson, is that "if a job has to be done to meet the needs of the people, and no one else can do it, then it is the proper function of the federal government."

Here we have, by prominent spokesmen of both political parties, an unqualified repudiation of the principle of limited government. There is no reference by either of them to the Constitution, or any attempt to define the legitimate functions of government. The government can do whatever *needs* to be done; note, too, the implicit but necessary assumption that it is the government itself that determines *what* needs to

be done. We must not, I think underrate the impor-
tance of these statements. They reflect the view of a
majority of the leaders of one of our parties, and of
a strong minority among the leaders of the other, and
they propound the first principle of totalitarianism:
that the State is competent to do all things and is
limited in what it actually does only by the will of
those who control the State.

It is clear that this view is in direct conflict with
the Constitution which is an instrument, above all,
for *limiting* the functions of government, and which
is as binding today as when it was written. But we
are advised to go a step further and ask why the
Constitution's framers restricted the scope of government. Conservatives are often charged, and in a sense
rightly so, with having an overly mechanistic view
of the Constitution: "It is America's enabling document; we are American citizens; therefore," the Conservatives' theme runs, "we are morally and legally
obliged to comply with the document." All true. But
the Constitution has a broader claim on our loyalty
than that. The founding fathers had a *reason* for en-
dorsing the principle of limited government; and this
reason recommends defense of the constitutional
scheme even to those who take their citizenship
obligations lightly. The reason is simple, and it lies
at the heart of the Conservative philosophy.

Throughout history, government has proved to be
the chief instrument for thwarting man's liberty. Gov-

ernment represents power in the hands of some men to control and regulate the lives of other men. And power, as Lord Acton said, *corrupts* men. "Absolute power," he added, "corrupts absolutely."

State power, considered in the abstract, need not restrict freedom: but absolute state power always does. The *legitimate* functions of government are actually conducive to freedom. Maintaining internal order, keeping foreign foes at bay, administering justice, removing obstacles to the free interchange of goods — the exercise of these powers makes it possible for men to follow their chosen pursuits with maximum freedom. But note that the very instrument by which these desirable ends are achieved *can* be the instrument for achieving undesirable ends—that government can, instead of extending freedom, restrict freedom. And note, secondly, that the "can" quickly becomes "will" the moment the holders of government power are left to their own devices. This is because of the corrupting influence of power, the natural tendency of men who possess *some* power to take unto themselves *more* power. The tendency leads eventually to the acquisition of *all* power — whether in the hands of one or many makes little difference to the freedom of those left on the outside.

Such, then, is history's lesson, which Messrs. Acheson and Larson evidently did not read: release the holders of state power from any restraints other than those they wish to impose upon themselves, and you are swinging down the well-travelled road to absolutism.

The framers of the Constitution had learned the lesson. They were not only students of history, but victims of it: they knew from vivid, personal experience that freedom depends on effective restraints against the accumulation of power in a single authority. And that is what the Constitution is: *a system of restraints against the natural tendency of government to expand in the direction of absolutism.* We all know the main components of the system. The first is the limitation of the federal government's authority to specific, delegated powers. The second, a corollary of the first, is the reservation to the States and the people of all power not delegated to the federal government. The third is a careful division of the federal government's power among three separate branches. The fourth is a prohibition against impetuous alteration of the system — namely, Article V's tortuous, but wise, amendment procedures.

Was it then a *Democracy* the framers created? Hardly. The system of restraints, on the face of it, was directed not only against individual tyrants, but also against a tyranny of the masses. The framers were well aware of the danger posed by self-seeking demagogues — that they might persuade a majority of the people to confer on government vast powers in return for deceptive promises of economic gain. And so they forbade such a transfer of power — first by declaring, in effect, that certain activities are outside the natural and legitimate scope of the public authority, and secondly by dispersing public authority among several levels and branches of government in the hope that each seat of authority, jealous of its own prerogatives, would have a natural incentive to resist aggression by the others.

But the framers were not visionaries. They knew that rules of government, however brilliantly calculated to cope with the imperfect nature of man, however carefully designed to avoid the pitfalls of power, would be no match for men who were determined to disregard them. In the last analysis their system of government would prosper only if the governed were sufficiently determined that it should. "What have you given us?" a woman asked Ben Franklin toward the close of the Constitutional Convention. "A Republic," he said, *if you can keep it!*"

We have not kept it. The Achesons and Larsons have had their way. The system of restraints has fallen into disrepair. The federal government has moved into every field in which it believes its services are needed. The state governments are either excluded from their rightful functions by federal preemption, or they are allowed to act at the sufferance of the federal government. Inside the federal government both the executive and judicial branches have roamed far outside their constitutional boundary lines. And all of these things have come to pass without regard to the amendment procedures prescribed by Article V. The result is a Leviathan, a vast national authority out of touch with the people, and out of their control. This monolith of power is bounded only by the will of those who sit in high places.

There are a number of ways in which the power of government can be measured.

One is the size of its financial operations. Federal spending is now approaching a hundred billion dollars a year (compared with three and one-half billion less than three decades ago.)

Another is the scope of its activities. A study recently conducted by the *Chicago Tribune* showed that the federal government is now the "biggest land owner, property manager, renter, mover and hauler, medical clinician, lender, insurer, mortgage broker, employer, debtor, taxer and spender in all history."

Still another is the portion of the peoples' earnings government appropriates for its own use: nearly a third of earnings are taken every year in the form of taxes.

A fourth is the extent of government interference in the daily lives of individuals. The farmer is told how much wheat he can grow. The wage earner is at the mercy of national union leaders whose great power is a direct consequence of federal labor legis-

lation. The businessman is hampered by a maze of
government regulations, and often by direct government competition. The government takes six per cent
of most payrolls in Social Security Taxes and thus
compels millions of individuals to postpone until later
years the enjoyment of wealth they might otherwise
enjoy today. Increasingly, the federal government sets
standards of education, health and safety.

How did it happen? How did our national government grow from a servant with sharply limited powers into a master with virtually unlimited power?

In part, we were swindled. There are occasions
when we have elevated men and political parties to
power that promised to restore limited government
and then proceeded, after their election, to expand the
activities of government. But let us be honest with
ourselves. Broken promises are not the major causes
of our trouble. *Kept* promises are. All too often we
have put men in office who have suggested spending
a little more on this, a little more on that, who have
proposed a new welfare program, who have thought
of another variety of "security." We have taken the
bait, preferring to put off to another day the recapture of freedom and the restoration of our constitutional system. We have gone the way of many a
democratic society that has lost its freedom by per-
suading itself that if "the people" rule, all is well.

The Frenchman, Alexis de Tocqueville, probably

the most clairvoyant political observer of modern times, saw the danger when he visited this country in the 1830's. Even then he foresaw decay for a society that tended to put more emphasis on its democracy than on its republicanism. He predicted that America would produce, not tyrants but "guardians." And that the American people would "console themselves for being in tutelage by the reflection that they have chosen their own guardians. Every man allows himself to be put in lead-strings, because he sees that it is not a person nor a class of persons, but the people at large that hold the end of his chain."

Our tendency to concentrate power in the hands of a few men deeply concerns me. We can be conquered by bombs or by subversion; but we can also be conquered by neglect — by ignoring the Constitution and disregarding the principles of limited government. Our defenses against the accumulation of unlimited power in Washington are in poorer shape, I fear, than our defenses against the aggressive designs of Moscow. Like so many other nations before us, we may succumb through internal weakness rather than fall before a foreign foe.

I am convinced that most Americans now want to reverse the trend. I think that concern for our vanishing freedoms is genuine. I think that the people's uneasiness in the stifling omnipresence of government has turned into something approaching alarm. But bemoaning the evil will not drive it back, and accusing fingers will not shrink government.

*The turn will come when we entrust the conduct of
our affairs to men who understand that their first
duty as public officials is to divest themselves of the
power they have been given.* It will come when Americans, in hundreds of communities throughout the nation, decide to put the man in office who is pledged
to enforce the Constitution and restore the Republic.
Who will proclaim in a campaign speech: "I have
little interest in streamlining government or in making it more efficient, for I mean to reduce its size.
I do not undertake to promote welfare, for I propose
to extend freedom. My aim is not to pass laws, but
to repeal them. It is not to inaugurate new programs,
but to cancel old ones that do violence to the Constitution, or that have failed in their purpose, or that
impose on the people an unwarranted financial burden. I will not attempt to discover whether legislation
is 'needed' before I have first determined whether it
is constitutionally permissible. And if I should later
be attacked for neglecting my constituents' 'interests,'
I shall reply that I was informed their main interest
is liberty and that in that cause I am doing the very
best I can."

CHAPTER THREE

States' Rights

The Governor of New York, in 1930, pointed out that the Constitution does not empower the Congress to deal with "a great number of . . . vital problems of government, such as the conduct of public utilities, of banks, of insurance, of business, of agriculture, of education, of social welfare, and a dozen other important features." And he added that "Washington must not be encouraged to interfere" in these areas.

Franklin Roosevelt's rapid conversion from Constitutionalism to the doctrine of unlimited government, is an oft-told story. But I am here concerned not so much by the abandonment of States' Rights by the national Democratic Party — an event that occurred some years ago when that party was captured by the Socialist ideologues in and about the labor movement — as by the unmistakable tendency of the Republican Party to adopt the same course. The result is that today *neither* of our two parties maintains a meaningful commitment to the principle of States' Rights. Thus, the cornerstone of the Republic, our chief bulwark against the encroachment of individual freedom by Big Government, is fast disappearing under the piling sands of absolutism.

The Republican Party, to be sure, gives lip-service to States' Rights. We often *talk* about "returning to the States their rightful powers"; the Administration has even gone so far as to sponsor a federal-state conference on the problem. But deeds are what count, and I regret to say that in actual practice, the Republican Party, like the Democratic Party, summons the coercive power of the federal government whenever national leaders conclude that the States are not performing satisfactorily.

Let us focus attention on one method of federal interference — one that tends to be neglected in much of the public discussion of the problem. In recent years the federal government has continued, and in many cases has increased, federal "grants-in-aid" to the States in a number of areas in which the Constitution recognizes the exclusive jurisdiction of the States. These grants are called "matching funds" and are designed to "stimulate" state spending in health, education, welfare, conservation or any other area in which the federal government decides there is a need for national action. If the States agree to put up money for these purposes, the federal government undertakes to match the appropriation according to a ratio prescribed by Congress. Sometimes the ratio is fifty-

fifty; often the federal government contributes over half the cost.

There are two things to note about these programs. The first is that they are *federal* programs — they are conceived by the federal government both as to purpose and as to extent. The second is that the "stimulative" grants are, in effect, a mixture of blackmail and bribery. The States are told to go along with the program "or else." Once the federal government has offered matching funds, it is unlikely, as a practical matter, that a member of a State Legislature will turn down his State's fair share of revenue collected from all of the States. Understandably, many legislators feel that to refuse aid would be political suicide. This is an indirect form of coercion, but it is effective nonetheless.

A more direct method of coercion is for the federal government to *threaten* to move in unless state governments take action that Washington deems appropriate. Not so long ago, for example, the Secretary of Labor gave the States a lecture on the wisdom of enacting "up-to-date" unemployment compensation laws. He made no effort to disguise the alternative: if the States failed to act, the federal government would.

Here are some examples of the "stimulative" approach. Late in 1957 a "Joint Federal-State Action Committee" recommended that certain matching funds programs be "returned" to the States on the scarcely disguised grounds that the States, in the view of the Committee, had learned to live up to their responsibilities. These are the areas in which the States were learning to behave: "vocational education" programs in agriculture, home economics, practical nursing, and the fisheries trade; local sewage projects; slum clearance and urban renewal; and enforcement of health and safety standards in connection with the atomic energy program.

Now the point is not that Congress failed to act on these recommendations, or that the Administration gave them only half-hearted support; but rather that the federal government had no business entering these fields in the first place, and thus had no business taking upon itself the prerogative of judging the States' performance. The Republican Party should have said this plainly and forthrightly and demanded the immediate withdrawal of the federal government.

We can best understand our error, I think, by examining the theory behind it. I have already alluded to the book, *A Republican Looks at His Party*, which is an elaborate rationalization of the "Modern Republican" approach to current problems. (It does the job just as well, I might add, for the Democrats' approach.) Mr. Larson devotes a good deal of space to the question of States' Rights. He contends that while there is "a general presumption" in favor of States' Rights, thanks to the Tenth Amendment, this presumption must give way whenever it appears to the federal authorities that the States are not responding satisfactorily to "the needs of the people." This is a paraphrase of his position but not, I think, an unjust one. And if this approach appears to be a high-handed way of dealing with an explicit constitutional provision, Mr. Larson justifies the argument by summoning the concept that "for every right there is a corresponding duty." "When we speak of States' Rights," he writes, "we should never forget to add that there go with those rights the corresponding States' responsibilities." Therefore, he concludes, if the States fail to do their duty, they have only themselves to blame when the federal government intervenes.

The trouble with this argument is that it treats the Constitution of the United States as a kind of handbook in political theory, to be heeded or ignored depending on how it fits the plans of contemporary federal officials. The Tenth Amendment is *not* "a general assumption," but a prohibitory rule of law. The Tenth Amendment recognizes the States' *jurisdiction* in certain areas. States' Rights means that the States have a right to act or *not to act,* as they see fit, in the areas reserved to them. The States may have duties corresponding to these rights, but the duties are owed to the people of the States, not to the federal government. Therefore, the recourse lies not with the federal government, which is not sovereign, but with the people who are, and who have full power to take disciplinary action. If the people are unhappy with say, their State's disability insurance program, they can bring pressure to bear on their state officials and, if that fails, they can elect a new set of officials. And if, in the unhappy event they should wish to divest themselves of this responsibility, they can amend the Constitution. The Constitution, I repeat, draws a sharp and clear line between federal jurisdiction and state jurisdiction. The federal government's failure to recognize that line has been a crushing blow to the principle of limited government.

But again, I caution against a defensive, or apologetic, appeal to the Constitution. There is a *reason* for its reservation of States' Rights. Not only does it prevent the accumulation of power in a central government that is remote from the people and relatively immune from popular restraints; it also recognizes the principle that essentially local problems are best dealt with by the people most directly concerned. Who knows better than New Yorkers how much and what kind of publicly-financed slum clearance in New York City is needed and can be afforded? Who knows better than Nebraskans whether that State has an adequate nursing program? Who knows better than Arizonans the kind of school program that is needed to educate their children? The people of my own State — and I am confident that I speak for the majority of them — have long since seen through the spurious suggestion that federal aid comes "free." They know that the money comes out of their own pockets, and that it is returned to them minus a broker's fee taken by the federal bureaucracy. They know, too, that the power to decide how that money shall be spent is withdrawn from them and exercised by some planning board deep in the caverns of one of the federal agencies. They understand this represents a great and perhaps irreparable loss — not only in their wealth, but in their priceless liberty.

Nothing could so far advance the cause of freedom as for state officials throughout the land to assert their rightful claims to lost state power; and for the federal government to withdraw promptly and totally from every jurisdiction which the Constitution reserved to the states.

CHAPTER FOUR

And Civil Rights

AN ATTEMPT has been made in recent years to disparage the principle of States' Rights by equating it with defense of the South's position on racial integration. I have already indicated that the reach of States' Rights is much broader than that—that it affects Northerners as well as Southerners, and concerns many matters that have nothing to do with the race question. Still, it is quite true that the integration issue is affected by the States' Rights principle, and that the South's position on the issue is, today, the most conspicuous expression of the principle. So much so that the country is now in the grips of a spirited and sometimes ugly controversy over an imagined conflict between States' Rights, on the one hand, and what are called "civil rights" on the other.

I say an imagined conflict because I deny that there *can* be a conflict between States' Rights, properly defined—and civil rights, properly defined. If States' "Rights" are so asserted as to encroach upon individual rights that are protected by valid federal laws, then the exercise of state power is a nullity. Conversely, if individual "rights" are so asserted as to infringe upon valid state power, then the assertion of those "rights" is a nullity. The rights themselves do not clash. The conflict arises from a failure to define the two categories of rights correctly, and to assert them lawfully.

States' Rights are easy enough to define. The Tenth Amendment does it succinctly: "The powers not delegated to the United States by the Constituion nor prohibited by it to the States are reserved to the States respectively, or to the people."

Civil rights should be no harder. In fact, however— thanks to extravagant and shameless misuse by people who ought to know better—it is one of the most badly understood concepts in modern political usage. Civil rights is frequently used synonymously with "human rights"—or with "natural rights." As often as not, it is simply a name for describing an activity that someone deems politically or socially desirable. A sociologist writes a paper proposing to abolish some inequity, or a politician makes a speech about it—and, behold, a new "civil right" is born! The Supreme Court has displayed the same creative powers.

A *civil* right is a right that is asserted and is therefore protected by some valid law. It may be asserted by the common law, or by local or federal statutes, or by the Constitution; *but unless a right is incorporated in the law, it is not a civil right and is not enforceable by the instruments of the civil law.* There may be some rights—"natural," "human," or otherwise—that *should* also be civil rights. But if we desire to give such rights the protection of the law, our recourse is to a legislature or to the amendment procedures of the Constitution. We must not look to politicians, or sociologists—or the courts—to correct the deficiency.

In the field of racial relations, there are some rights that are clearly protected by valid laws and are therefore "civil" rights. One of them is the right to vote. The Fifteenth Amendment provides that no one shall be denied the franchise on account of race, color or previous condition of servitude. Similarly with certain legal privileges enforced by the Fourteenth Amendment. The legislative history of that amendment makes it clear (I quote from the Civil Rights Act of 1866 which the Amendment was designed to legitimize) that people of all races shall be equally entitled "to make and enforce contracts, to sue, be parties, and give evidence, to inherit, to purchase, lease, sell, hold and convey real and personal property and to full and equal benefit of all laws and proceedings for the security of persons and property." After the passage of that Act and the Amendment, all persons, Negroes included, had a "civil" right to these protections.

It is otherwise let us note, with education. For the federal Constitution does *not* require the States to maintain racially mixed schools. Despite the recent holding of the Supreme Court, I am firmly convinced —not only that integrated schools are not required— but that the Constitution does not permit any interference whatsoever by the federal government in the field of education. It may be just or wise or expedient for negro children to attend the same schools as white children, but they do not have a civil right to do so which is protected by the federal constitution, or which is enforceable by the federal government.

The intentions of the founding fathers in this matter are beyond any doubt: *no powers regarding education were given the federal government.* Consequently, under the Tenth Amendment, jurisdiction over the entire field was reserved to the States. The remaining question is whether the Fourteenth Amendment—concretely, that amendment's "equal protection" clause—modified the original prohibition against federal intervention.

To my knowledge it has never been seriously argued—the argument certainly was not made by the Supreme Court—that the authors of the Fourteenth Amendment intended to alter the Constitutional scheme with regard to education. Indeed, in the famous school integration decision, *Brown v. Board of Education* (1954), the Supreme Court justices expressly acknowledged that they were not being guided by the intentions of the amendment's authors. *"In approaching this problem,"* Chief Justice Warren said *"we cannot turn the clock back to 1868 when the amendment was adopted . . . We must consider public education in the light of its full development and in its present place in American life throughout the nation."* In effect, the Court said that what matters is not the ideas of the men who wrote the Constitution, but the *Court's* ideas. It was only by engrafting its own views onto the established law of the land that the Court was able to reach the decision it did.

The intentions of the Fourteenth Amendment's authors are perfectly clear. Consider these facts. 1. During the entire congressional debate on the Fourteenth Amendment it was never once suggested by any proponent of the amendment that it would outlaw segregated schools. 2. At the same time that it approved the Fourteenth Amendment, Congress established schools in Washington in Georgetown "for the sole use of . . . colored children." 3. In all the debates on the amendment by the State Legislatures there was only one legislator, a man in Indiana, who thought the amendment would affect schools 4. The great majority of the States that approved the amendment permitted or required segregated schools at the very time they approved the amendment. There is not room here for exhaustive treatment of this evidence, but the facts are well documented, and they are all we have to know about the Fourteenth Amendment's bearing on this problem. The amendment was not intended to, and therefore it did not outlaw racially separate schools. It was not intended to, and therefore it did not, authorize *any* federal intervention in the field of education.

I am therefore not impressed by the claim that the Supreme Court's decision on school integration is the law of the land. *The Constitution, and the laws "made in pursuance thereof," are the "supreme law of the land."* The Constitution is what its authors intended it to be and said it was—not what the Supreme Court says it is. If we condone the practice of substituting our own intentions for those of the Constitution's framers, we reject, in effect, the principle of Constitutional Government: we endorse a rule of men, not of laws.

I have great respect for the Supreme Court as an institution, but I cannot believe that I display that respect by submitting abjectly to abuses of power by the Court, and by condoning its unconstitutional trespass into the legislative sphere of government. The Congress and the States, equally with the Supreme Court, are obliged to interpret and comply with the Constitution according to their own lights. I therefore support all efforts by the States, excluding violence of course, to preserve their rightful powers over education.

As for the Congress, I would hope that the national legislature would help clarify the problem by proposing to the States a Constitutional amendment that would reaffirm the States' exclusive jurisdiction in the field of education. This amendment would, in my judgment, assert what is already provided unmistakably by the Constitution; but it would put the matter beyond any further question.

It so happens that I am in agreement with the *objectives* of the Supreme Court as stated in the *Brown* decision. I believe that it *is* both wise and just for negro children to attend the same schools as whites, and that to deny them this opportunity carries with it strong implications of inferiority. I am not prepared, however, to impose that judgment of mine on the people of Mississippi or South Carolina, or to tell them what methods should be adopted and what pace should be kept in striving toward that goal. That is their business, not mine. I believe that the problem of race relations, like all social and cultural problems, is best handled by the people directly concerned. Social and cultural change, however desirable, should not be effected by the engines of national power. Let us, through persuasion and education, seek to improve institutions we deem defective. But let us, in doing so, respect the orderly processes of the law. Any other course enthrones tyrants and dooms freedom.

CHAPTER FIVE

Freedom for the Farmer

"... supervision of agriculture and other concerns of a similar nature ... which are proper to be provided for by local legislation, can never be desirable cares of a general jurisdiction. It is therefore improbable that there should exist a disposition in the federal councils to usurp the powers with which they are connected; because the attempt to exercise those powers would be as troublesome as they were nugatory." Alexander Hamilton in the Federalist Papers, No. 17.

HAMILTON WAS WRONG in his prediction as to what men would do, but quite right in foreseeing the consequences of their foolhardiness. Federal intervention in agriculture has, indeed, proved "troublesome." Disregard of the Constitution in this field has brought about the inevitable loss of personal freedom; and it has created economic chaos. Unmanageable surpluses, an immense tax burden, high consumer prices, vexatious controls—I doubt if the folly of ignoring the principle of limited government has ever been more convincingly demonstrated.

We have blundered on so grand a scale that even our critical faculties seem to have been damaged in the process. No man who is familiar with the subject will deny that the policy of price supports and production controls has been a colossal failure. Yet, today, some of our best minds have no better solution to the problem than to raise the supports and increase the controls!

The teaching of the Constitution on this matter is perfectly clear. *No power over agriculture was given to any branch of the national government.* The sponsors of the first Agriculture Adjustment Act, passed in 1933, tried to justify the law under the so-called general welfare clause of the Constitution. The Supreme Court promptly struck down that legislation on the grounds that the phrase, "general welfare," was simply a qualification of the taxing power and did not give Congress the power to *control* anything. "The regulation (of agricultural production)," the Court said in United States v. Butler (1936) "is not in fact voluntary. The farmer, of course, may refuse to comply [a privilege not given him under present legislation], but the price of such refusal is loss of benefits . . . the power to confer or withhold unlimited benefits is the power to coerce or destroy . . ."

The New Deal Congress replied by enacting substantially identical legislation, the second AAA, and now sought to justify the program as a "regulation of interstate commerce." This was a transparent evasion of the Butler case; but the Supreme Court, which by this time was under heavy political fire for having thrwarted the "Roosevelt Revolution," made one of its celebrated about-faces and upheld the new act. The federal government has usurped many powers under the guise of "regulating commerce," but this instance of distorting the plain meaning of the Constitution's language is perhaps the most flagrant on record.

In the case that upheld the second AAA, *Wickard* v. *Filburn*, (1942), a farmer had been fined for planting 23 acres of wheat, instead of the eleven acres the government had allotted him—notwithstanding that the "excess" wheat had been consumed *on his own farm*. Now how in the world, the farmer wanted to know, can it be said that the wheat I feed my own stock is in interstate commerce? That's easy, the Court said. If you had *not* used your own wheat for feed, you might have bought feed from someone else, and that purchase might have affected the price of wheat that *was* transported in interstate commerce! By this bizarre reasoning the Court made the commerce clause as wide as the world and nullified the Constitution's clear reservation to the States of jurisdiction over agriculture.

The tragedy, of course, is that the federal government's unconstitutional intrusion into Agriculture has not brought us any closer to a solution of the "farm problem." The problem, when federal intervention began, was declining farm incomes. Today, many farm incomes are still low. But now we have additional problems—production controls that restrict freedom, high consumer prices, huge crop surpluses and a gigantic tax bill that is running close to six billion dollars a year. No matter what variant of the price support-production control approach we adopt, the solution to these problems continues to elude us.

The reason government intervention has created more problems than it has solved is quite simple. *Farm production, like any other production is best controlled by the natural operation of the free market.* If the nation's farmers are permitted to sell their produce freely, at price consumers are willing to pay, they will, under the law of supply and demand, end up producing roughly what can be consumed in national and world markets. And if farmers, in general, find they are not getting high enough prices for their produce, some of them will move into other kinds of economic activity. The result will be reduced agricultural production and higher incomes for those who remain on the farms. If, however, the government interferes with this natural economic process, and pegs prices higher than the consumer is willing to pay, the result will be, in Hamilton's phrase, "troublesome." The nation will pay exorbitant prices for work that is not needed and for produce that cannot be consumed.

In recent years, the government has sought to alleviate the problem of over-production by the soil bank and acreage retirement programs. Actually, these programs are simply a modern version of the hog-killing and potato-burning schemes promoted by Henry Wallace during the New Deal. And they have been no more successful in reducing surpluses than their predecessors. But there is also a positive evil in these programs: in effect, they reward people *for not producing*. For a nation that is expressing great concern over its "economic growth," I cannot conceive of a more absurd and self-defeating policy than one which subsidizes non-production.

The problem of surpluses will not be solved until we recognize that technological progress and other factors have made it possible for the needs of America, and those of accessible world markets, to be satisfied by a far fewer number of farmers than now till the soil. I cannot believe that any serious student of the farm problems fails to appreciate this fact. What has been lacking is not an understanding of a problem that is really quite impossible not to understand, but the political courage to do something about it.

Doing something about it means—and there can be no equivocation here—*prompt and final termination of the farm subsidy program.* The only way to persuade farmers to enter other fields of endeavor is to stop paying inefficient farmers for produce that cannot be sold at free market prices. Is this a cruel solution? Is it heartless to permit the natural laws of economics to determine how many farmers there shall be in the same way that those laws determine how many bankers, or druggists, or watchmakers there shall be? It was never considered so before the subsidy program began. Let us remember that the movement *from* the farm *to* other fields of endeavor has been proceeding in this country since its beginning—and with good effects, not ill.

I cannot believe that this course will lose politicians as many votes as some of them seem to fear. Most farmers want to stand on their own feet. They are prepared to take their chances in the free market. They have a more intimate knowledge than most of us of the consequences of unlimited government power, and so, it would seem, a greater interest than most in returning agriculture to freedom and economic sanity.

CHAPTER SIX

Freedom for Labor

If I had to select the vote I regard as the most important of my Senate career it would be the one I cast on the Kennedy-Ervin "Labor Reform" Bill of 1959. The Senate passed the measure 90-1; the dissenting vote was mine. The measure had been advertised as a cure-all for the evils uncovered by the McClellan Committee investigation. I opposed it because I felt certain that legislation which pretended to respond to the popular demand for safeguards against union power, but actually did not do so, would preclude the possibility of meaningful legislation for some time to come.

That opinion was vindicated later on. The House of Representatives rejected Kennedy-Ervin, and substituted in its place a much better measure, the Landrum-Griffin bill. The ensuing conference between representatives of the two houses made only minor changes in the House version; I would guess that 90% of the original Landrum-Griffin bill survived in the conferees' report. The Senate adopted the report with only two dissenting votes—proof to me that my initial protest had been wise.

But the protest still holds: though the Landrum-Griffin Bill was an improvement over the Kennedy measure, Congress has still to come to grips with the real evil in the Labor field. Graft and corruption are symptoms of the illness that besets the labor movement, not the cause of it. *The cause is the enormous economic and political power now concentrated in the hands of union leaders.*

Such power hurts the nation's economy by forcing on employers contract terms that encourage inefficiency, lower production and high prices—all of which result in a lower standard of living for the American people.

It corrupts the nation's political life by exerting undue influence on the selection of public officials.

It gravely compromises the freedom of millions of individual workers who are able to register a dissent against the practice of union leaders only at the risk of losing their jobs.

All of us have heard the charge that to thus criticize the power of Big Labor is to be anti-labor and anti-union. This is an argument that serves the interest of union leaders, but it does not usually fit the facts, and it certainly does not do justice to my views. I believe that unionism, kept within its proper and natural bounds, accomplishes a positive good for the country. Unions *can* be an instrument for achieving economic justice for the working man. Moreover, they are an alternative to, and thus discourage State Socialism. Most important of all, they are an expression of freedom. Trade unions properly conceived, is an expression of man's inalienable right to associate with other men for the achievement of legitimate objectives.

The natural function of a trade union and the one for which it was historically conceived is to represent those employees who want collective representation in bargaining with their employers over terms of employment. But note that this function is perverted the moment a union claims the right to represent employees who do not want representation, *or* conducts activities that have nothing to do with terms of employment (e.g. political activities), *or* tries to deal with an industry as a whole instead of with individual employers.

As America turned increasingly, in the latter half of the nineteenth century, from an agricultural nation into an industrial one, and as the size of business enterprises expanded, individual wage earners found themselves at a distinct disadvantage in dealing with their employers over terms of employment. The economic power of the large enterprises, as compared with that of the individual employee, was such that wages and conditions of employment were pretty much what the employer decided they would be. Under these conditions, as a means of increasing their economic power, many employees chose to band together and create a common agent for negotiating with their employers.

As time went on, we found that the working man's right to bargain through a collective agent needed legal protection; accordingly Congress enacted laws—notably certain provisions of the Clayton Act, the Norris LaGuardia Act and the Wagner Act—to make sure that employees would be able to bargain collectively.

This is not the place to examine those laws in detail. It is clear, however, that they have *over*-accomplished their purpose. Thanks to some unwise provisions and to the absence of others that should have been included, the delicate balance of power we sought to achieve between labor and management has shifted, in avalanche proportions, to labor's advantage. Or, more correctly to the advantage of union leaders. This mammoth concentration of power in the hands of a few men is, I repeat, a grave threat to the nation's economic stability, and to the nation's political processes. More important, it has taken from the individual wage earner a large portion of his freedom.

The time has come, not to abolish unions or deprive them of deserved gains; but to redress the balance— to restore unions to their proper role in a free society.

We have seen that unions perform their natural function when three conditions are observed: association with the union is voluntary; the union confines its activities to collective bargaining; the bargaining is conducted with the employer of the workers concerned. Let us briefly treat with each of these conditions, noting the extent to which they are violated today, and the remedial action we are called upon to take.

Freedom of Association. Here the argument is so plain that I wonder why elaboration is necessary. What could be more fundamental than the freedom to associate with other men, or not to associate, as each man's conscience and reason dictates? Yet compulsory unionism is the rule rather than the exception today in the ranks of organized labor. Millions of laboring men are required to join the union that is the recognized bargaining agent at the place they work. Union shop agreements deny to these laboring men the right to decide for themselves what union they will join, or indeed, whether they will join at all. The exercise of freedom for many of these citizens, means the loss of their jobs.

Here is the kind of thing that can happen as the result of compulsory unionism. X, a family man in Pennsylvania had been a union member in good standing for over twenty years. When the United Electrical Workers became the recognized bargaining agent at his plant, he refused to join on the grounds the UEW was Communist dominated—a judgment that had been made by the CIO itself when it expelled the UEW in

1950. The result, since his employer had a union shop agreement with the UEW, was that X lost his job.

The remedy here is to give freedom of association legal protection. And that is why I strongly favor enactment of State right-to-work laws which forbid contracts that make union membership a condition of employment. These laws are aimed at removing a great blight on the contemporary American scene, and I am at a loss to understand why so many people who so often profess concern for "civil rights" and "civil liberties" are vehemently opposed to them. Freedom of association is one of the natural rights of man. Clearly, therefore, it should also be a "civil" right. Right-to-work laws derive from the natural law: they are simply an attempt to give freedom of association the added protection of civil law.

I am well aware of the "free loader" argument, so often advanced by union leaders in defense of compulsory unionism. The contention is that a man ought not to enjoy the benefits of an organization's activities unless he contributes his fair share of their cost. I am unaware, however, of any other organization or institution that seeks to enforce this theory by compulsion. The Red Cross benefits all of us, directly or indirectly, but *no one suggests that Red Cross donations be compulsory.* It is one thing to say that a man *should* contribute to an association that is purportedly acting in his interest; it is quite another thing to say that he *must* do so. I believe that a man ought to join a union if it is a good union that is serving the interests of its members. I believe, moreover, that most men *will* give support to a union *provided it is deserving of that support.* There will always be some men, of course, who will try to sponge off others; but let us not express our contempt for *some* men by denying freedom of choice to *all* men.

The union leaders' further argument that right to work legislation is a "union-busting" device is simply not borne out by the facts. A recent survey disclosed that *in all of the nineteen States which have enacted right-to-work laws union membership increased after the right-to-work laws were passed.* It is also well to remember that the union movement throughout the world has prospered when it has been put on a voluntary basis. Contrary to popular belief compulsory unionism is not typical of the labor movement in the free world. It prevails in the United States and England, but in the other countries of Western Europe and in Australia, union membership is generally on a voluntary basis. Indeed the greatest percentage of unionized workers are found in countries that prohibit compulsion by law. The unions in those countries operate on the principle that a union is stronger and better if its members give their adherence of their own free will.

Here, it seems to me, is the sensible way to combat graft and corruption in the labor movement. As long as union leaders can *force* workers to join their organization, they have no incentive to act responsibly. But if workers could choose to belong or not to belong depending on how the union performed, the pressure to stamp out malpractice would become irresistible. If unions had to earn the adherence of their members the result would be—not only more freedom for the working man—but much less dishonesty and high handedness in the management of the union affairs.

Political Freedom. One way we exercise political freedom is to vote for the candidate of our choice. Another way is to use our money to try to persuade other voters to make a similar choice—that is, to contribute to our candidate's campaign. If either of these freedoms is violated, the consequences are very grave not only for the individual voter and contributor, but for the society whose free political processes depend on a wide distribution of political power.

It is in the second of these areas, that of political contributions, that labor unions seriously compromise American freedom. They do this by spending the money of union members without prior consultation for purposes the individual members may or may not approve of, purposes that are decided upon by a relatively small number of union leaders. Probably the greatest spender in the labor movement is the powerful AFL/CIO Committee on Political Education (COPE) which is supported in its "educational" work entirely by union general funds.

It is impossible to say just how much unions spend on political campaigns; certainly one can't tell from the amounts officially reported, which invariably present a grossly distorted picture. In 1956, for example, Labor officially acknowledged expenditures of $941,-271. According to that official report, $79,939 of the total was spent in the State of Michigan. However, a Senate investigating committee obtained evidence that in that year each of Michigan's 700,000 union members had been assessed $1.20 as a contribution to a "citizenship fund," and that this money was made available for political activities. This suggests that labor spent, from that one source alone, almost a million dollars in Michigan instead of $79,000. By projecting the difference on a nation-wide scale we get a more realistic idea of the size of Labor's political contributions.

Union political activity is not confined, of course, to direct financial contributions. In fact, this is one of its smallest endeavors. Unions provide manpower for election day chores—for making phone calls, driving cars, manning the polls and so on. Often the union members who perform these chores are reimbursed for their time-off out of union funds. Unions also sponsor radio and television programs and distribute a huge volume of printed material designed to support the candidate of the union's choice. In short, they perform all the functions of a regular party organization.

Now the evil here is twofold. For one thing, the union's decision whether to support candidate X or candidate Y—whether to help the Republican Party or the Democratic Party—is not reached by a poll of the union membership. It is made by a handful of top union officers. These few men are thus able to wield tremendous political power in virtue of their ability to spend other people's money. No one else in America is so privileged.

The other evil is more serious. Individual union members are denied the right to decide for themselves how to spend their money. Certainly a moral issue is at stake here. *Is it morally permissible to take the money of a Republican union member, for example, and spend it on behalf of a Democrat?* The travesty is deeper, of course, when the money takes the form of compulsory union dues. Under union shop conditions, the only way an individual can avoid contributing to the political campaign of a candidate whom he may not approve is to give up his job.

The passage of right-to-work laws will help the situation. But putting unionism on a voluntary basis is only part of the answer. For even though a man can leave or refuse to join a union that spends money for purposes that he does not approve, there may be other factors that would dissuade him from doing so. In many communities strong economic and social pressures are exerted on behalf of joining a union—quite aside from the threat of loss of employment. As a result, a man may decide to join a union notwithstanding his disapproval of its political activities. And the question remains: Should that man's union dues be used for political purposes? The answer is clearly, no. Unions exist, presumably to confer economic advantages on their members, not to perform political services for them. Unions should therefore be forbidden to engage in any kind of political activity. I believe that the Federal Corrupt Practices Act *does* forbid such activity. That legislation has been circumvented by the "education" approach and other devices; and Congress and the courts, in effect, have looked the other way. The only remedy, it appears is new legislation.

In order to achieve the widest possible distribution of political power, financial contributions to political campaigns should be made by individuals and individuals alone. I see no reason for labor unions—or corporations—to participate in politics. Both were created for economic purposes and their activities should be restricted accordingly.

Economic Freedom. Americans have been much disturbed in recent years by the apparent power of Big Labor to impose its will on the nation's economic life whenever the impulse strikes. The recent steel controversy, and the terms of its settlement, are the latest illustration of Labor's ability to get its way notwithstanding the cost to the rest of society. When the strike began, neutral observers—including government economists normally friendly to the unions—agreed that the Steel Workers' wage demands were exorbitant and would inevitably cause further inflation; and that the steel companies were quite right in insisting that certain "work rules" promoted inefficiency and retarded production. Nevertheless, the steel companies were forced to accept a settlement that postponed indefinitely revision of work rules and granted a large portion of the union's wage demands.

The reason the union won is quite simple: it posed to the country the choice of tolerating stoppages in steel production that would imperil national security, or of consenting to an abandonment of the collective bargaining process. Since neither the steel companies nor the country at large wanted to resort to compulsory arbitration, the alternative was to give the unions what they asked. In this situation, the only power superior to union power was government power, and the government chose to yield.

One way to check the unions' power is for the government to dictate through compulsory arbitration, the terms of employment throughout an entire industry. I am opposed to this course because it simply transfers economic power from the unions to the government, and encourages State Socialism. The other way is to disperse union power and thus extend freedom in labor-management relations.

Eighty years ago the nation was faced with a comparable concentration of economic power. Large corporations, by gaining monopoly control over entire industries, had nullified the laws of competition that are conducive to freedom. We responded to that challenge by outlawing monopolies through the Sherman Act and other anti-trust legislation. *These laws, however, have never been applied to labor unions.* And I am at a loss to understand why. If it is wrong for a single corporation to dictate prices throughout an entire industry, it is also wrong for a single union—or, as is the actual case, a small number of union leaders—to dictate wages and terms of employment throughout an entire industry.

The evil to be eliminated is the power of unions to enforce industry-wide bargaining. Employees have a right, as we have seen, to select a common agent for bargaining with *their* employer but they do not have a right to select a national agent to bargain with all employers in the industry. If a union has the power to enforce uniform conditions of employment throughout the nation its power is comparable to that of a Socialist government.

Employers are forbidden to act collusively for sound reasons. The same reasons apply to unions. Industry-wide price-fixing causes economic dislocations? So does industry-wide wage-fixing. A wage that is appropriate in one part of the country may not be in another area where economic conditions are very different. Corporate monopolies impair the operation of the free market, and thus injure the consuming public. So do union monopolies. When the United Automobile Workers demand a wage increase from the auto industry, a single monolith is pitted against a number of separate, competing companies. The contest is an unequal one, for the union is able to play off one company against another. The result is that individual companies are unable to resist excessive wage demands and must, in turn, raise their prices. The consumer ultimately suffers for he pays prices that are fixed not by free market competition—the law of supply and demand—but by the arbitrary decision of national union leaders. Far better if the employees of Ford were required to deal with Ford, and those of Chrysler with Chrysler and so on. The collective bargaining process will work for the common good in all industries if it is confined to the employers and employees directly concerned.

Let us henceforth make war on all monopolies — whether corporate or union. The enemy of freedom is unrestrained power, and the champions of freedom will fight against the concentration of power wherever they find it.

CHAPTER SEVEN

Taxes and Spending

We all have heard much throughout our lifetimes, and seen little happen, on the subject of high taxes. Where is the politician who has not promised his constituents a fight to the death for lower taxes—and who has not proceeded to vote for the very spending projects that make tax cuts impossible? There are some the shoe does not fit, but I am afraid not many. Talk of tax reduction has thus come to have a hollow ring. The people listen, but do not believe. And worse: as the public grows more and more cynical, the politician feels less and less compelled to take his promises seriously.

I suspect that this vicious circle of cynicism and failure to perform is primarily the result of the Liberals' success in reading out of the discussion the moral principles with which the subject of taxation is so intimately connected. We have been led to look upon taxation as merely a problem of public financing: How much money does the government need? We have been led to discount, and often to forget altogether, the bearing of taxation on the problem of individual freedom. We have been persuaded that the government has an unlimited claim on the wealth of the people, and that the only pertinent question is what portion of its claim the government should exercise. The American taxpayer, I think, has lost confidence in *his* claim to his money. He has been handicapped in resisting high taxes by the feeling that he is, in the nature of things, obliged to accommodate whatever need for his wealth government chooses to assert.

The "nature of things," I submit, is quite different. Government does *not* have an unlimited claim on the earnings of individuals. One of the foremost precepts of the natural law is man's right to the possession and the use of his property. And a man's earnings are his property as much as his land and the house in which he lives. Indeed, in the industrial age, earnings are probably the most prevalent form of property. It has been the fashion in recent years to disparage "property rights"—to associate them with greed and materialism. This attack on property rights is actually an attack on freedom. It is another instance of the modern failure to take into account the *whole* man. How can a man be truly free if he is denied the means to exercise freedom? How can he be free if the fruits of his labor are not his to dispose of, but are treated, instead, as part of a common pool of public wealth? Property and freedom are inseparable: to the extent government takes the one in the form of taxes, it intrudes on the other.

THE CONSCIENCE OF A CONSERVATIVE

Here is an indication of how taxation currently in-
fringes on our freedom. A family man earning $4,500
a year works, on the average, twenty-two days a
month. Taxes, visible and invisible, take approximately 32% of his earnings. This means that one-third, or
seven whole days, of his monthly labor goes for taxes.
The average American is therefore working one-third
of the time for government: a third of what he produces is not available for his own use but is confiscat-
ed and used by others who have not earned it. Let us
note that by this measure the United States is already
one-third "socialized." The late Senator Taft made the
point often. "You can socialize," he said "just as well
by a steady increase in the burden of taxation beyond
the 30% we have already reached as you can by government seizure. The very imposition of heavy taxes
is a limit on a man's freedom."

But having said that each man has an inalienable
right to his property, it also must be said that every
citizen has an obligation to contribute his fair share to
the legitimate functions of government. Government,
in other words, has *some* claim on our wealth, and the
problem is to define that claim in a way that gives due
consideration to the property rights of the individual.

The size of the government's rightful claim—that is,
the total amount it may take in taxes—will be determined by how we define the "legitimate functions of
government." With regard to the federal government,
the *Constitution* is the proper standard of legitimacy:

its "legitimate" powers, as we have seen are those the Constitution has delegated to it. Therefore, if we adhere to the Constitution, the federal government's total tax bill will be the cost of exercising such of its *delegated* powers as our representatives deem necessary in the national interest. But conversely, when the federal government enacts programs that are *not* authorized by its delegated powers, the taxes needed to pay for such programs *exceed* the government's rightful claim on our wealth.

The distribution of the government's claim is the next part of the definition. What is a "fair share?" I believe that the requirements of justice here are perfectly clear: *government has a right to claim an equal percentage of each man's wealth, and no more.* Property taxes are typically levied on this basis. Excise and sales taxes are based on the same principle—though the tax is levied on a transaction rather than on property. *The principle is equally valid with regard to incomes, inheritances and gifts.* The idea that a man who makes $100,000 a year should be forced to contribute ninety per cent of his income to the cost of government, while the man who makes $10,000 is made to pay twenty per cent is repugnant to my notions of justice. I do not believe in punishing success. To put it more broadly, I believe it is contrary to the natural right to property to which we have just alluded—and is therefore immoral—to deny to the man whose labor has produced more abundant fruit than that of his neighbor the opportunity of enjoying the abundance he has created. As for the claim that the government *needs* the graduated tax for revenue purposes, the facts are to the contrary. The total revenue collected from income taxes beyond the twenty per cent level amounts to less than $5 billion—less than the federal government now spends on the one item of agriculture.

The graduated tax is a *confiscatory* tax. Its effect, and to a large extent its aim, is to bring down all men to a common level. Many of the leading proponents of the graduated tax frankly admit that their purpose is to redistribute the nation's wealth. Their aim is an egalitarian society—an objective that does violence both to the charter of the Republic and the laws of Nature. We are all equal in the eyes of God but we are equal *in no other respect*. Artificial devices for enforcing equality among unequal men must be rejected if we would restore that charter and honor those laws.

One problem with regard to taxes, then, is to enforce justice—to abolish the graduated features of our tax laws; and the sooner we get at the job, the better.

The other, and the one that has the greatest impact on our daily lives, is to reduce the volume of taxes. And this takes us to the question of government spending. While there is something to be said for the proposition that spending will never be reduced so long as there is money in the federal treasury, I believe that as a practical matter spending cuts must come before tax cuts. If we reduce taxes before firm, principled decisions are made about expenditures, we will court deficit spending and the inflationary effects that invariably follow.

It is in the area of spending that the Republican Party's performance, in its seven years of power, has been most disappointing.

In the Summer of 1952, shortly after the Republican Convention, the two men who had battled for the Presidential nomination met at Morningside Heights, New York, to discuss the problem of taxes and spending. After the conference, Senator Taft announced: "General Eisenhower emphatically agrees with me in the proposal to reduce drastically overall expenses. Our goal is about $70 billion in fiscal 1954 (President Truman had proposed $81 billion) and $60 billion in fiscal 1955 . . . Of course, I hope we may do better than that and that the reduction can steadily continue." Thereafter, the idea of a $60 billion budget in 1955, plus the promise of further reductions later on, became an integral part of the Republican campaign.

Now it would be bad enough if we had simply failed to redeem our promise to reduce spending; the fact, however, is that federal spending has greatly *increased* during the Republican years. Instead of a $60 billion budget, we are confronted, in fiscal 1961, with a budget of approximately $80 billion. If we add to the formal budget figure disbursements from the so-called trust funds for Social Security and the Federal Highway Program—as we must if we are to obtain a realistic picture of federal expenditures — total federal spending will be in the neighborhood of *$95 billion.*

We are often told that increased federal spending is simply a reflection of the increased cost of national defense. This is untrue. In the last ten years purely *domestic* expenditures have increased from $15.2 billion, in fiscal 1951, to a proposed $37.0 billion in fiscal 1961*
—*an increase of 143%!* Here are the figures measured by a slightly different yardstick: during the last five years of the Truman Administration the average annual federal expenditure for domestic purposes was $17.7 billion; during the last five years of the Eisenhower Administration it was $33.6 billion, an increase of 89%.

Some allowance must be made, of course, for the increase in population; obviously the same welfare program will cost more if there are more people to be cared for. But the increase in population does not begin to account for the increase in spending. During the ten-year period in which federal spending will have increased by 143%, our population will have increased by roughly 18%. Nor does inflation account for the difference. In the past ten years the value of the dollar has decreased less than 20%. Finally, we are often told that the government's *share* of total spending in the country is what is important and consequently we

*These figures do not include interest payments on the national debt.

must take into account the increase in gross national product. Again, however, the increase in GNP, which was roughly 40% over the past ten years, is not comparable to a 143% increase in federal spending. The conclusion here is inescapable—that far from arresting federal spending and the trend toward Statism we Republicans have kept the trend moving forward.

I do not mean to suggest, of course, that things would have been different under a Democratic Administration. Every year the Democratic national leadership demands that the federal government spend *more* than it is spending, and that Republicans propose to spend. *And this year, several weeks before President Eisenhower submitted his 1961 budget, The Democratic National Advisory Council issued a manifesto calling for profligate spending increases in nearly every department of the federal government; the demands for increases in domestic spending alone could hardly cost less than $20 billion a year.*

I do mean to say, however, that *neither* of our political parties has seriously faced up to the problem of government spending. The recommendations of the Hoover Commission which could save the taxpayer in the neighborhood of $7 billion a year have been largely ignored. Yet even these recommendations, dealing as they do for the most part with extravagance and waste, do not go to the heart of the problem. The root evil is that the government is engaged in activities in which it has no legitimate business. As long as the federal government acknowledges responsibility in a given social or economic field, its spending in that field cannot be substantially reduced. As long as the federal government acknowledges responsibilty for education, for example, the amount of federal aid is bound to increase, at the very least, in direct proportion to the cost of supporting the nation's schools. *The only way to curtail spending substantially, is to eliminate the programs on which excess spending is consumed.*

The government must begin to *withdraw* from a whole series of programs that are outside its constitutional mandate—from social welfare programs, education, public power, agriculture, public housing, urban renewal and all the other activities that can be better performed by lower levels of government or by private institutions or by individuals. I do not suggest that the federal government drop all of these programs overnight. But I do suggest that we establish, by law, a rigid timetable for a staged withdrawal. We might provide, for example, for a 10% spending reduction each year in all of the fields in which federal participation is undesirable. It is only through this kind of determined assault on the principle of unlimited government that American people will obtain relief from high taxes, and will start making progress toward regaining their freedom.

And let us, by all means, remember the *nation's* interest in reducing taxes and spending. The need for "economic growth" that we hear so much about these days will be achieved, not by the government harnessing the nation's economic forces, but by emancipating them. By reducing taxes and spending we will not only return to the individual the means with which he can assert his freedom and dignity, but also guarantee to the nation the economic strength that will always be its ultimate defense against foreign foes.

CHAPTER EIGHT

The Welfare State

Washington—The President estimated that the expenditures of the Department of Health, Education
and Welfare in the fiscal year 1961 (including Social Security payments) would exceed $15,000,-
000,000. Thus the current results of New Deal legislation are Federal disbursements for human welfare
in this country second only to national defense.

The *New York Times*, January 18, 1960, p. 1.

FOR MANY YEARS it appeared that
the principal domestic threat to our freedom was contained in the doctrines of Karl Marx. The collectivists
—non-Communists as well as Communists—had adopted the Marxist objective of "socializing the means of
production." And so it seemed that if collectivization
were imposed, it would take the form of a State owned
and operated economy. I doubt whether this is the
main threat any longer.

The collectivists have found, both in this country
and in other industrialized nations of the West, that

free enterprise has removed the economic and social
conditions that might have made a class struggle
possible. Mammoth productivity, wide distribution of
wealth, high standards of living, the trade union movement—these and other factors have eliminated whatever incentive there might have been for the "proletar-
iat" to rise up, peaceably or otherwise, and assume direct ownership of productive property. Significantly,
the bankruptcy of doctrinaire Marxism has been expressly acknowledged by the Socialist Party of West
Germany, and by the dominant faction of the Socialist
Party of Great Britain. In this country the abandonment of the Marxist approach (outside the Communist
Party, of course) is attested to by the negligible
strength of the Socialist Party, and more tellingly
perhaps, by the content of left wing literature and by
the programs of left wing political organizations such
as the Americans For Democratic Action.

The currently favored instrument of collectivization
is the Welfare State. The collectivists have not abandoned their ultimate goal—to subordinate the individual to the State—but their strategy has changed. They
have learned that Socialism can be achieved through
Welfarism quite as well as through Nationalization.
They understand that private property can be confis-
cated as effectively by taxation as by expropriating it.
They understand that the individual can be put at the
mercy of the State—not only by making the State his
employer—but by divesting him of the means to provide for his personal needs and by giving the State the

responsibility of caring for those needs from cradle to grave. Moreover, they have discovered—and here is the critical point—that *Welfarism is much more compatible with the political processes of a democratic society.* Nationalization ran into popular opposition, but the collectivists feel sure the Welfare State can be erected by the simple expedient of buying votes with promises of "free" federal benefits—"free" housing, "free" school aid, "free" hospitalization, "free" retirement pay and so on . . . The correctness of this estimate can be seen from the portion of the federal budget that is now allocated to welfare, an amount second only to the cost of national defense.*

I do not welcome this shift of strategy. Socialism-through-Welfarism poses a far greater danger to freedom than Socialism-through-Nationalization precisely because it *is* more difficult to combat. The evils of Nationalization are self-evident and immediate. Those of Welfarism are veiled and tend to be postponed. People can understand the consequences of turning over ownership of the steel industry, say, to the State; and they can be counted on to oppose such a proposal. But let the government increase its contribution to the "Public Assistance" program and we will, at most, grumble about excessive government spending. The effect of Welfarism on freedom will be felt later on—after its beneficiaries have become its victims, after dependence on

---

*The total figure is substantially higher than the $15,000,000,000 noted above if we take into account welfare expenditures outside the Department of Health, Education and Welfare—for federal housing projects, for example.

government has turned into bondage and it is too late
to unlock the jail.

But a far more important factor is Welfarism's
strong emotional appeal to many voters, and the con-
sequent temptations it presents the average politician.
It is hard, as we have seen, to make out a case for
State ownership. It is very different with the rhetoric
of humanitarianism. How easy it is to reach the voters
with earnest importunities for helping the needy. And
how difficult for Conservatives to resist these demands
without appearing to be callous and contemptuous of
the plight of less fortunate citizens. Here, perhaps, is
the best illustration of the failure of the Conservative
demonstration.

I know, for I have heard the questions often. Have
you no sense of social obligation? the Liberals ask.
Have you no concern for people who are out of work?
for sick people who lack medical care? for children in
overcrowded schools? Are you unmoved by the problems of the aged and disabled? Are you *against* human
welfare?

The answer to all of these questions is, of course, no.
But a simple "no" is not enough. I feel certain that
Conservatism is through unless Conservatives can
demonstrate and communicate the difference between
being concerned with these problems and believing
that the federal government is the proper agent for
their solution.

The long range political consequences of Welfarism are plain enough: as we have seen, the State that is able to deal with its citizens as wards and dependents has gathered unto itself unlimited political and economic power and is thus able to rule as absolutely as any oriental despot.

Let us, however, weigh the consequences of Welfarism on the individual citizen.

Consider, first, the effect of Welfarism on the donors of government welfare—not only those who pay for it but also the voters and their elected representatives who decide that the benefits shall be conferred. Does some credit redound on them for trying to care for the needs of their fellow citizens? Are they to be commended and rewarded, at some moment in eternity, for their "charity?" I think not. Suppose I should vote for a measure providing for free medical care: I am unaware of any moral virtue that is attached to my decision to confiscate the earnings of X and give them to Y.

Suppose, however, that X approves of the program —that he has voted for welfarist politicians with the idea of helping his fellow man. Surely the wholesomeness of his act is diluted by the fact that he is voting not only to have his own money taken but also that of his fellow citizens who may have different ideas about their social obligations. Why does not such a man, instead, contribute what he regards as his just share of human welfare to a private charity?

Consider the consequences to the recipient of welfarism. For one thing, he mortgages himself to the federal government. In return for benefits—which, in the majority of cases, he pays for—he concedes to the government the ultimate in political power—the power to grant or withhold from him the necessities of life as the government sees fit. Even more important, however, is the effect on him—the elimination of any feeling of responsibility for his own welfare and that of his family and neighbors. A man may not immediately, or ever, comprehend the harm thus done to his character. Indeed, this is one of the great evils of Welfarism—that it transforms the individul from a dignified, industrious, self-reliant *spiritual* being into a dependent animal creature without his knowing it. There is no avoiding this damage to character under the Welfare State. Welfare programs cannot help but promote the idea that the government *owes* the benefits it confers on the individual, and that the individual is entitled, by right, to receive them. Such programs are sold to the country precisely on the argument that government has an *obligation* to care for the needs of its citizens. Is it possible that the message will reach those who vote for the benefits, but not those who receive them? How different it is with private charity where both the giver and the receiver understand that charity is the product of the humanitarian impulses of the giver, not the due of the receiver.

Let us, then, not blunt the noble impulses of mankind by reducing charity to a mechanical operation of the federal government. Let us, by all means, encourage, those who are fortunate and able to care for the needs of those who are unfortunate and disabled. But let us do this in a way that is conducive to the spiritual as well as the material well-being of our citizens—and in a way that will preserve their freedom. Let welfare be a private concern. Let it be promoted by individuals and families, by churches, private hospitals, religious service organizations, community charities and other institutions that have been established for this purpose. If the objection is raised that private institutions lack sufficient funds, let us remember that every penny the federal government does *not* appropriate for welfare is potentially available for private use—and without the overhead charge for processing the money through the federal bureaucracy. Indeed, high taxes, for which government Welfarism is so largely responsible, is the biggest obstacle to fund raising by private charities.

Finally, if we deem public intervention necessary, let the job be done by local and state authorities that are incapable of accumulating the vast political power that is so inimical to our liberties.

The Welfare State is *not* inevitable, as its proponents are so fond of telling us. There is nothing inherent in an industrialized economy, or in democratic processes of government that *must* produce de Tocqueville's "guardian society." Our future, like our past, will be what we make it. And we can shatter the collectivists' designs on individual freedom if we will impress upon the men who conduct our affairs this one truth: that the material and spiritual sides of man are intertwined; that it is impossible for the State to assume responsibility for one without intruding on the essential nature of the other; that if we take from a man the personal responsibility for caring for his material needs, we take from him also the will and the opportunity to be free.

CHAPTER NINE

Some Notes on Education

I agree with lobbyists for federal school aid that education is one of the great problems of our day. I am afraid, however, that their views and mine regarding the nature of the problem are many miles apart. They tend to see the problem in *quantitative* terms — not enough schools, not enough teachers, not enough equipment. I think it has to do with *quality*: How good are the schools we have? Their solution is to spend more money. Mine is to raise standards. Their recourse is to the federal government. Mine is to the local public school board, the private school, the individual citizen—as far away from the federal government as one can possibly go. And I suspect that if we knew which of these two views on education will eventually prevail, we would know also whether Western civilization is due to survive, or will pass away.

To put this somewhat differently, I believe that our ability to cope with the great crises that lie ahead will be enhanced in direct ratio as we recapture the lost art of learning, and will diminish in direct ratio as we give

responsibility for training our children's minds to the
federal bureaucracy.

But let us put these differences aside for the moment and note four reasons why federal aid to education is objectionable even if we grant that the problem
is primarily quantitative.

The first is that federal intervention in education is
unconstitutional. It is the fashion these days to say
that responsibility for education "traditionally" rests
with the local community—as a prelude to proposing
an exception to the tradition in the form of federal aid.
This "tradition," let us remember, is also the *law*. It is
sanctioned by the Constitution of the United States,
for education is one of the powers reserved to the
States by the Tenth Amendment. Therefore, any federal aid program, however desirable it might appear,
must be regarded as illegal until such time as the Constitution is amended.

The second objection is that the alleged need for
federal funds has never been convincingly demonstrated. It all depends, of course, on how the question is
put. If you ask, Does State X need additional educational facilities? the answer may be yes. But if you ask,
Does State X require additional facilities that are beyond the the reach of its own financial means? the answer is invariably no. The White House Conference on
Education in 1955 was, most of us will remember, an
elaborate effort to demonstrate popular support for

federal aid. As expected, the "consensus" of the conference was that more federal aid was needed. However, the conferees reached another conclusion that was hardly noticed by the press. "No state represented," the Conference report stated, "has a demonstrated financial incapacity to build the schools they will need during the next five years." What is lacking, the report went on, *is not money, but a "political determination powerful enough to overcome all the obstacles."*

Through the succeeding five years, congressional committees have listened to hundreds of hours of testimony in favor of federal aid, but they have never heard that 1955 finding successfully contradicted. What the White House conferees were saying in 1955, and what proponents of federal aid to education have been saying ever since, is that because a few States have not seen fit to take care of their school needs, it is incumbent upon the federal government to take up the slack. My view is that if State X possesses the wealth to educate its children adequately, but has failed to utilize its wealth for that purpose, it is up to the people of State X to take remedial action through their local and state governments. The federal government has neither the right nor the duty to intervene.

Let us, moreover, keep the problem in proper perspective. The national school system is *not* in distress. Shortly before the Senate debate this year on increased federal aid, I asked Mr. Arthur Flemming the Sec-

retary of Health, Education and Welfare, how many
of the Nation's school districts were in actual trouble
—how many, that is, had reached their bonded limit.
His answer was approximately 230. Now there are
roughly 42,000 school districts in America. Thus, proponents of federal aid are talking about a problem that
affects only one-half of one per cent of our school districts! I cannot believe that the state governments responsible for those areas are incapable of making up
whatever deficiencies exist. It so happens that the
same deficiency figure—one-half of one per cent—ap-
plies to my own state of Arizona. And Arizona proudly
turned down federal funds under the 1958 National
Defense Education Act on the grounds that Arizonans,
themselves, were quite capable of closing the gap.

This may be the place, while we are speaking of
need, to lay to rest the notion that the American people have been niggardly in support of their schools.
Since the end of World War II, Americans have built
550,000 classrooms at a cost of approximately $19 bil-
lion—almost all of which was raised at the local level.
This new construction provided space for over 15 million pupils during a period when the school population increased by only 10 million pupils. It is evident,
therefore, that increased school expenditures have
more than kept pace with increased school needs.

Here are some of the figures. In the school year
1949-50 there were 25 million students enrolled in various education institutions in the United States. In the

year 1959-60 there were 34.7 million—an increase of 38%. During the same period revenues for school use, raised largely at the local level, increased from 5.4 billion to 12.1 billion—an increase of 124%. When school expenditures increase three and a half times as fast as the school population, I do not think that the adequacy of America's "traditional" approach to education is open to serious question.

The third objection to federal aid is that it promotes the idea that federal school money is "free" money, and thus gives the people a distorted picture of the cost of education. I was distressed to find that five out of six high school and junior college students recently interviewed in Phoenix said they favored federal aid because it would mean more money for local schools and ease the financial burden on Arizona taxpayers.

The truth, of course, is that the federal government has no funds except those it extracts from the taxpayers who reside in the various States. The money that the federal government pays to State X for education has been taken from the citizens of State X in federal taxes and comes back to them, minus the Washington brokerage fee. The less wealthy States, to be sure, receive slightly more than they give, just as the more wealthy States receive somewhat less. But the differences are negligible. For the most part, federal aid simply substitutes the tax-collecting facilities of the federal government for those of local governments. This fact cannot be stressed often enough; for stripped of the idea that federal money is free money, federal aid to education is exposed as an act of naked compulsion—a decision by the federal government to force the people of the States to spend more money than they choose to spend for this purpose voluntarily.

The fourth objection is that federal aid *to* education inevitably means federal control *of* education. For many years, advocates of federal aid denied that aid implies control, but in the light of the National Defense Education Act of 1958 they cannot very well maintain their position. Federal aid under the act is conditioned upon compliance by the States and local educational institutions with various standards and specifications laid down by the Department of Health, Education and Welfare. *There are no less than twelve direct controls of this kind in the act.* Moreover, the acknowledged purpose of the act is to persuade local educational institutions to put greater emphasis on the physical sciences and other subjects directly related to national defense. I do not question the desirability of encouraging increased proficiency in the physical sciences, but when the federal government does the encouraging through the withholding and granting of funds, I do not see how it can be denied that the federal government is helping to determine the *content* of education; and influencing content is the last, not the first, stage of control.

Nobody should be surprised that aid has led to controls. It could, and *should not* be otherwise. Congress

cannot be expected to appropriate the people's money
and make no provision for how it will be spent. Congress would be shirking its responsibilities to the taxpayer if it distributed his money willy-nilly, without
regard to its use. Should Congress permit the use of
federal funds to subsidize Communist schools and thus
promote the cause of our enemies? Of course not. But a
prohibition of such use is clearly an exercise of federal
control. Congress will always feel impelled to establish conditions under which people's money is to be
spent, and while some controls may be wise we are not
guaranteed against unwise controls any more than we
are guaranteed against unwise Congressmen. The mistake is not the controls but appropriating the money
that requires controls.

So much for the evils and dangers of federal aid.
Note that I have not denied that many of our children
are being inadequately educated, or that the problem
is nation-wide. I have only denied that it is the kind of
problem that requires a solution at the national level.
To the extent the problem is quantitative—to the extent we have too few classrooms and pay some of our
teachers too little money—the shortages can be taken
care of by the localities concerned. But more: to the
extent the problem is qualitative—which in my opinion it mainly is—it is manifestly one that lends itself
to correction at the local level. There is no place where
deficiencies in the *content* of an educational system
can be better understood than locally where a com-

munity has the opportunity to view and judge the product of its own school system.

In the main, the trouble with American education is that we have put into practice the educational philosophy expounded by John Dewey and his disciples. In varying degrees we have adopted what has been called "progressive education."

Subscribing to the egalitarian notion that every child must have the same education, we have neglected to provide an educational system which will tax the talents and stir the ambitions of our best students and which will thus insure us the kind of leaders we will need in the future.

In our desire to make sure that our children learn to "adjust" to their environment, we have given them insufficient opportunity to acquire the knowledge that will enable them to *master* their environment.

In our attempt to make education "fun," we have neglected the academic disciplines that develop sound minds and are conducive to sound characters.

Responding to the Deweyite attack on methods of teaching, we have encouraged the teaching profession to be more concerned with *how* a subject is taught than with *what* is taught. Most important of all: in our anxiety to "improve" the world and insure "progress" we have permitted our schools to become laboratories for social and economic change according to the predilections of the professional educators. We have forgotten that the proper function of the school is to transmit the cultural heritage of one generation to the next generation, and to so train the minds of the new generation as to make them capable of absorbing ancient learning and applying it to the problem of its own day.

The fundamental explanation of this distortion of values is that we have forgotten that purpose of education. Or better: we have forgotten for *whom* education is intended. The function of our schools is not to educate, or elevate, *society;* but rather to educate *individuals* and to equip them with the knowledge that will enable them to take care of society's needs. We have forgotten that a society progresses only to the extent that it produces leaders that are capable of guiding and inspiring progress. And we cannot develop such leaders unless our standards of education are geared to excellence instead of mediocrity. We must give full rein to individual talents, and we must encourage our schools to enforce the academic disciplines —to put preponderant emphasis on English, mathematics, history, literature, foreign languages and the natural sciences. We should look upon our schools— not as a place to train the "whole character" of the child—a responsibility that properly belongs to his family and church—but to train his *mind*.

Our country's past progress has been the result, not of the mass mind applying average intelligence to the problems of the day, but of the brilliance and dedication of wise individuals who applied their wisdom to advance the freedom and the material well-being of all of our people. And so if we would improve education in America—and advance the fortunes of freedom —we will not rush to the federal treasury with requests for money. We will focus attention on our local community, and make sure that our schools, private and public, are performing the job the Nation has the right to expect of them.

CHAPTER TEN

The Soviet Menace

AND STILL the awful truth remains: We can establish the domestic conditions for maximizing freedom, along the lines I have indicated, and yet become slaves. We can do this by losing the Cold War to the Soviet Union.

American freedom has always depended, to an extent, on what is happening beyond our shores. Even in Ben Franklin's day, Americans had to reckon with foreign threats. Our forebearers knew that "keeping a Republic" meant, above all, keeping it safe from foreign transgressors; they knew that a people cannot live and work freely, and develop national institutions conducive to freedom, except in peace and with independence. In those early days the threat to peace and independence was very real. We were a fledgling-nation and the slightest misstep—or faint hearts—would have laid us open to the ravages of predatory European powers. It was only because wise and courageous men understood that defense of freedom required risks and

sacrifice, as well as their belief in it, that we survived
the crisis of national infancy. As we grew stronger,
and as the oceans continued to interpose a physical
barrier between ourselves and European militarism,
the foreign danger gradually receded. Though we always had to keep a weather eye on would-be con-
querors, our independence was acknowledged and
peace, unless we chose otherwise, was established. Indeed, after the Second World War, we were not only
master of our own destiny; we were master of the
world. With a monopoly of atomic weapons, and with
a conventional military establishment superior to any
in the world, America was—in relative and absolute
terms—the most powerful nation the world had ever
known. American freedom was as secure as at any
time in our history.

Now, a decade and half later, we have come full
circle and our national existence is once again threat-
ened as it was in the early days of the Republic.
Though we are still strong physically, we are in clear
and imminent danger of being overwhelmed by alien
forces. We are confronted by a revolutionary world
movement that possesses not only the will to dominate absolutely every square mile of the globe, but increasingly the capacity to do so: a military power that
rivals our own, political warfare and propaganda skills
that are superior to ours, an international fifth column
that operates conspiratorially in the heart of our defenses, an ideology that imbues its adherents with a
sense of historical mission; and all of these resources

controlled by a ruthless despotism that brooks no deviation from the revolutionary course. This threat, moreover, is growing day by day. And it has now reached the point where American leaders, both political and intellectual, are searching desperately for means of "appeasing" or "accommodating" the Soviet Union as the price of national survival. The American people are being told that, however valuable their freedom may be, it is even more important to live. A craven fear of death is entering the American consciousness; so much so that many recently felt that honoring the chief despot himself was the price we had to pay to avoid nuclear destruction.

The temptation is strong to blame the deterioration of America's fortunes on the Soviet Union's acquisition of nuclear weapons. But this is self-delusion. The rot had set in, the crumbling of our position was already observable, long before the Communists detonated their first Atom Bomb. Even in the early 1950s, when America still held unquestioned nuclear superiority, it was clear that we were losing the Cold War. Time and again in my campaign speeches of 1952 I warned my fellow Arizonans that "American Foreign Policy has brought us from a position of undisputed power, in seven short years, to the brink of possible disaster." And in the succeeding seven years, that trend, because its cause remains, has continued.

The real cause of the deterioration can be simply stated. Our enemies have understood the nature of the conflict, and we have not. They are determined to win the conflict, and we are not.

I hesitate to restate the obvious—to say again what has been said so many times before by so many others: that the Communists' aim is to conquer the world. I repeat it because it is the beginning and the end of our knowledge about the conflict between East and West. I repeat it because I fear that however often we have given lip-service to this central political fact of our time, very few of us have *believed* it. If we had, our entire approach to foreign policy over the past fourteen years would have been radically different, and the course of world events radically changed.

If an enemy power is bent on conquering you, and proposes to turn all of his resources to that end, he is at war with you; and you—unless you contemplate surrender—are at war with him. Moreover—unless you contemplate treason—your objective, like his, will be victory. Not "peace," but victory. Now, while traitors (and perhaps cowards) have at times occupied key positions in our government, it is clear that our national leadership over the past fourteen years has favored neither surrender nor treason. It is equally clear, however, that our leaders have not made *victory* the goal of American policy. And the reason that they have not done so, I am saying, is that they have never believed deeply that the Communists are in earnest.

Our avowed national objective is "peace." We have,

with great sincerity, "waged" peace, while the Communists wage war. We have sought "settlements," while the Communists seek victories. We have tried to pacify the world. The Communists mean to own it. Here is why the contest has been an unequal one, and why, essentially, we are losing it.

Peace, to be sure, is a proper goal for American policy—as long as it is understood that peace is not all we seek. For we do not want the peace of surrender. We want a peace in which freedom and justice will prevail, and that—given the nature of Communism— is a peace in which Soviet power will no longer be in a position to threaten us and the rest of the world. A tolerable peace, in other words, must *follow* victory over Communism. We have been fourteen years trying to bury that unpleasant fact. It cannot be buried and any foreign policy that ignores it will lead to our extinction as a nation.

We do not, of course, want to achieve victory by force of arms. If possible, overt hostilities should always be avoided; especially is this so when a shooting war may cause the death of many millions of people, including our own. But we cannot, for that reason, make the avoidance of a shooting war our chief objective. If we do that—if we tell ourselves that it is more important to avoid shooting than to keep our freedom— we are committed to a course that has only one terminal point: surrender. We cannot, by proclamation, make war "unthinkable." For it is not unthinkable to the Communists: naturally, they would prefer to avoid war, but they are prepared to risk it, in the last analysis, to achieve their objectives. We must, in our hearts, be equally dedicated to our objectives. If war is unthinkable to us but not to them, the famous "balance of terror" is not a balance at all, but an instrument of blackmail. U. S.-Soviet power may be in balance; but if we, and not they, rule out the possibility of using that power, the Kremlin can create crisis after crisis, and force the U. S., because of our greater fear of war, to back down every time. And it cannot be long before a universal Communist Empire sits astride the globe.

The rallying cry of an appeasement organization, portrayed in a recent novel on American politics, was "I would rather crawl on my knees to Moscow than die under an Atom bomb." This sentiment, of course, repudiates everything that is courageous and honorable and dignified in the human being. We must—as the first step toward saving American freedom—affirm the contrary view and make it the cornerstone of our foreign policy: that we would rather die than lose our freedom. There are ways which I will suggest later on—not easy ways, to be sure—in which we may save both our freedom *and* our lives; but all such suggestions are meaningless and vain unless we first understand what the objective is. We want to stay alive, of course; but more than that we want to be free. We want to have peace; but before that we want to establish the conditions that will make peace tolerable.

"Like it or not," Eugene Lyons has written, "the great and inescapeable task of our epoch is not to end the Cold War but to win it."

I suggest that we look at America's present foreign policy, and ask whether it is conducive to victory. There are several aspects of this policy. Let us measure each of them by the test: Does it help defeat the enemy?

DEFENSIVE ALLIANCES Through NATO, SEATO and the Central Treaty Organization in mid-Asia, we have served notice on the Kremlin that overt Communist aggression in certain areas of the world will be opposed by American arms. It is likely that the existence of these alliances has helped discourage military adventurism by the Communists.

Still, we should not overestimate the value of the alliances. Though they play a significant role in safeguarding American freedom, there are a number of reasons why it is a limited role.

First, the alliance system is not co-extensive with the line that must be held if enemy expansion is to be prevented. There are huge areas of the non-Communist world that the alliances do not touch. Nor— even assuming America is strong enough to guard a world-wide defense perimeter—is there any prospect of bringing these areas into the system. The so-called neutral countries of the Middle East, Africa and South-

ern Asia have refused to align themselves with the
anti-Communist cause, and it is in those areas, as we
might expect, that the Communists are making significant strides. This is a critical weakness. If all of
those areas should fall under Communist rule, the
alliances would be outflanked everywhere: the system would be reduced to a series of outposts, and probably indefensible ones at that, in a wholly hostile
world.

Secondly, the alliance system does not protect even
its members against the most prevalent kind of Communist aggression: political penetration and internal
subversion. Iraq is a case in point. We had pledged
ourselves to support the Iraqi against overt Soviet
aggression—not only under the Baghdad Pact of which
Iraq was the cornerstone, but also under the Eisenhower Doctrine. Iraq fell victim to a pro-Communist
coup without an American or Russian shot being fired.
Cuba is another example. If the Red Army had landed
in Havana, we would have come to Cuba's aid. Castro's
forces, however, were native Cubans; as a result, a
pro-Communist regime has become entrenched on our
very doorstep through the technique of internal subversion. And so it will always be with an enemy that
lays even more emphasis on political warfare than on
military warfare. So it will be until we learn to meet
the enemy on his own grounds.

But thirdly, the alliance system cannot adequately
protect its members even against *overt* aggression. In

the past, the Communists have been kept in check by America's strategic air arm. Indeed, in the light of the weakness of the allied nations' conventional military forces, our nuclear superiority has been the alliances' only real weapon. But as the Soviet Union draws abreast of us in nuclear strength, that weakness could prove our undoing. In a nuclear stalemate, where neither side is prepared to go "all out" over local issues, the side with the superior conventional forces has an obvious advantage. Moreover, it is clear that we cannot hope to match the Communist world man for man, nor are we capable of furnishing the guns and tanks necessary to defend thirty nations scattered over the face of the globe. The long-overdue answer, as we will see later on, lies in the development of a nuclear capacity for limited wars.

Finally—and I consider this the most serious defect of all—the alliance system is completely defensive in nature and outlook. This fact, in the light of the Communists' dynamic, offensive strategy, ultimately dooms it to failure. No nation at war, employing an exclusively defensive strategy, can hope to survive for long. Like the boxer who refuses to throw a punch, the defense-bound nation will be cut down sooner or later. As long as every encounter with the enemy is fought on his initiative, on grounds of his choosing and with weapons of his choosing, we shall keep on losing the Cold War.

FOREIGN AID Another aspect of our policy is the Foreign Aid program. To it, in the last fourteen years, we have committed over eighty billions of American treasure—in grants, loans, material, and technical assistance. I will not develop here what every thinking American knows about this Gargantuan expenditure—that it has had dire consequences, not only for the American taxpayer, but for the American economy; that it has been characterized by waste and extravagance both overseas and in the agencies that administer it; and that it has created a vast reservoir of anti-Americanism among proud peoples who, however irrationally, resent dependence on a foreign dole. I would rather put the question, Has the Foreign Aid program, for all of its drawbacks, made a compensating contribution toward winning the Cold War?

And this test, let me say parenthetically, is the only one under which the Foreign Aid program can be justified. It cannot, that is to say, be defended as a charity. The American government does not have the right, much less the obligation, to try to promote the economic and social welfare of foreign peoples. Of course, all of us are interested in combating poverty and disease wherever it exists. *But the Constitution does not empower our government to undertake that job in foreign countries,* no matter how worthwhile it might be. Therefore, except as it can be shown to promote America's national interests, the Foreign Aid program is unconstitutional.

It can be argued, but not proved, that American aid helped prevent Western Europe from going Communist after the Second World War. It is true, for example, that the Communist parties in France and Italy were somewhat weaker after economic recovery than before it. But it does not follow that recovery *caused* the reduction in Communist strength, or that American aid caused the recovery. It is also true, let us remember, that West Germany recovered economically at a far faster rate than France or Italy, and received comparatively little American aid.

It also can be argued that American military aid has made the difference between friendly countries having the power to fight off or discourage Communist aggression, and not having that power. Here, however, we must distinguish between friendly countries that were *not* able to build their own military forces, and those that were. Greece, Turkey, Free China, South Korea and South Vietnam needed our help. Other countries, England and France, for example, were able to maintain military forces with their own resources. For many years now, our allies in Western Europe have devoted smaller portions of their national budgets to military forces than we have. The result is that the American people, in the name of *military* aid, have been giving an *economic* handout to these nations; we have permitted them to transfer to their domestic economy funds which, in justice, should have been used in the common defense effort.

Now let us note a significant fact. In each of the situations we have mentioned so far — situations where some evidence exists that Foreign Aid has promoted American interests—there is a common denominator: *in every case, the recipient government was already committed to our side.* We *may* have made these nations, on balance, stronger and more constant allies, though even that is debatable. But we did not cause them to alter their basic political commitments. This brings us to the rest of the Foreign Aid program —and to the great fallacy that underlies it.

Increasingly, our foreign aid goes not to our friends, but to professed neutrals—and even to professed enemies. We furnish this aid under the theory that we can buy the allegiance of foreign peoples—or at least discourage them from "going Communist"—by making them economically prosperous. This has been called the "stomach theory of Communism," and it implies that a man's politics are determined by the amount of food in his belly.

Everything we have learned from experience, and from our observation of the nature of man, refutes this theory. A man's politics are, primarily, the product of his mind. Material wealth can help him further his political goals, but it will not change them. The fact that some poor, illiterate people have "gone Communist" does not prove that poverty caused them to do so any more than the fact that Alfred K. and Martha D. Stern are Communists proves that great wealth

and a good education make people go Communist.
Let us remember that Communism is a political movement, and that its weapons are primarily political.
The movement's effectiveness depends on small cadres
of political activists, and these cadres are, typically,
composed of literate and well-fed people. We are not
going to change the minds of such political activists,
or impede their agitation of the masses by a "war on
poverty," however worthy such an effort might be
on humanitarian grounds.

It thus makes little sense to try to promote anti-
Communism by giving money to governments that
are not anti-Communist, that are, indeed, far more
inclined to the Soviet-type society than to a free
one. And let us remember that the foreign policies of
many of the allegedly neutral nations that receive our
aid are not "neutral" at all. Is Sukarno's Indonesia
neutral when it encourages Red Chinese aggression?
Or Nehru's India when it censures the Western effort
to recover Suez but refuses to censure the Soviet in-
vasion of Hungary? Or Nasser's United Arab Republic
which equips its armed forces with Communist weapons and Communist personnel? Is American aid likely to make these nations less pro-Communist? Has it?

But let us, for the moment, concede the validity of
the "stomach theory," and ask a further question: Is
our foreign aid program the kind that will bring prosperity to underdeveloped countries? We Americans
believe—and we can cite one hundred and fifty years

of experience to support the belief—that the way to
build a strong economy is to encourage the free play
of economic forces: free capital, free labor, a free
market. Yet every one of the "neutral" countries we
are aiding is committed to a system of State Socialism.
Our present policy of government-to-government aid
strengthens Socialism in those countries. We are not
only perpetuating the inefficiency and waste that always attends government-controlled economies; by
strengthening the hand of those governments, we are
making it more difficult for free enterprise to take
hold. For this reason alone, we should eliminate all
government-to-government capital assistance and encourage the substitution of American private invest-
ment.

Our present Foreign Aid program, in sum, is not
only ill-administered, but ill-conceived. It has not, in
the majority of cases, made the free world stronger; it
has made America weaker; and it has created in minds
the world over an image of a nation that puts prime
reliance, not on spiritual and human values, but on the
material things that are the stock-in-trade of Communist propaganda. To this extent we have adopted
Communist doctrine.

In the future, if our methods are to be in tune with
our true objectives, we will confine foreign aid to military and technical assistance to those nations that
need it and that are committed to a common goal of
defeating world Communism.

NEGOTIATIONS As I write, the world is waiting for another round of diplomatic conferences between East and West. A full scale summit meeting is scheduled for Spring; later on, President Eisenhower and Premier Khrushchev will have further talks in the Soviet Union. And we are told that this is only the beginning of a long-range American policy to try to settle world problems by "negotiation."

As the preparations for the Spring meetings go forward, I am struck by a singular fact: no one on our side claims—let alone believes—that the West will be stronger after these new negotiations than it is today. The same was true last Summer. We agreed to "negotiate" about Berlin—not because we hoped to gain anything by such talks—but because the Communists had created a "crisis," and we could think of nothing better to do about it than go to the conference table. After all, we assured ourselves, there is no harm in talking.

I maintain there *is* harm in talking under present conditions. There are several reasons why this is so. First of all, Communists do not look upon negotiations, as we do, as an effort to reach an agreement. For them, negotiations are simply an *instrument* of political warfare. For them, a summit meeting is another battle in the struggle for the world. A diplomatic conference, in Communist language, is a "propaganda

forum from which to speak to the masses over the
heads of their leaders."

Of course, if the Communists can obtain a formal
agreement beneficial to them, so much the better. But
if not the negotiations themselves will provide victory
enough. For example, when the Soviets challenged
our rights in West Berlin, we handed them a victory
by the mere act of sitting down at the conference
table. By agreeing to negotiate on that subject, we
agreed that our rights in Berlin were "negotiable"—
something they never were before. Thus we acknowledged, in effect, the inadequacy of our position, and
the world now expects us to adjust it as proof of our
good faith. Our answer to Khrushchev's ultimatum
should have been that the status of West Berlin concerns only West Berliners and the occupying powers,
and is therefore not a matter that we are prepared to
discuss with the Soviet Union. That would have been
the end of the Berlin "crisis."

The Berlin situation illustrates another reason why
the West is at an inherent disadvantage in negotiating
with the Communists. The central strategic fact of the
Cold War, as it is presently fought, is that the Communists are on the offensive and we are on the defensive. The Soviet Union is always moving ahead, always trying to get something from the free world; the
West endeavors, at best, to hold what it has. Therefore, the focal point of negotiations is invariably some-
where in the non-Communist world. Every conference

between East and West deals with some territory or right belonging to the free world which the Communists covet. Conversely, since the free world does not seek the liberation of Communist territory, the possibility of Communist concessions never arises. Once the West did attempt to use the conference table for positive gain. At Geneva, in 1955, President Eisenhower told the Soviets he wanted to discuss the status of the satellite nations of Eastern Europe. He was promply advised that the Soviet Union did not consider the matter a legitimate subject for negotiation, and that was that. Now since we are not permitted to talk about what *we* can get, the only interesting question at an East-West conference is what the Communists can get. Under such conditions, we can never win. At best we can hope for a stalemate that will place us exactly where we started.

There is still another reason for questioning the value of negotiations. Assume that somehow we achieve an agreement we think advances our interests. Is there any reason for supposing the Communists will keep it one moment longer than suits their purpose? We, and they, are different in this respect. We keep our word. The long and perfidious Communist record of breaking agreements and treaties proves that the Soviet Union will not keep any agreement that is not to its advantage to keep. It follows that the only agreement worth making with the Soviets is one that will be self-enforceable—which means one that is in the Kremlin's interest to keep. But if that is the

case, why bother to "negotiate" about it? If an action
is in the interest of the Soviet Union, the Kremlin will
go ahead and perform it without feeling any need to
make it the subject of a formal treaty.

The next time we are urged to rush to the conference table in order to "relax world tensions," let our
reaction be determined by this simple fact: the only
"tensions" that exist between East and West have
been created, and deliberately so, by the Communists.
They can therefore be "relaxed" by the Kremlin's uni-
lateral act. The moment we decide to relax tensions by
a "negotiated compromise" we have decided to yield
something of value to the West.

THE "EXCHANGE"   In recent months, the so-called ex-
PROGRAM   change program has become an
                      increasingly prominent feature of
American foreign policy. The program began modest-
ly enough in 1955 at the Geneva Summit Meeting,
when we agreed with the Soviets to promote "cultural
exchanges" between the two countries. Since then we
have exchanged everything from opera companies and
basketball teams to trade exhibitions and heads of
governments. We are told that these exchanges are
our best hope of peace—that if only the American and
Russian peoples can learn to "understand" each other,
they will be able to reconcile their differences.

The claim that the conflict between the Soviets and
ourselves stems from a "lack of understanding" is one

of the great political fables of our time. *Whose* lack of understanding?

Are the American people ill-informed as to the nature of Communism and of the Soviet state? True, some Americans fail to grasp how evil the Soviet system really is. But a performance by the Bolshoi Ballet, or a tour of the United States by Nikita Khrushchev, is certainly not calculated to correct *that* deficiency.

What of the Soviet leaders? Are *they* misled? All of the evidence is that the men in the Kremlin have a greater knowledge of America than many of our own leaders. They know about our political system, our industrial capacity, our way of life—and would like to destroy it all.

What about the Russian people? We are repeatedly told that the Russian man-on-the-street is woefully ignorant of the American way, and that our trade exhibition in Moscow, for example, contributed vastly to his knowledge and thus to his appreciation of America. Assume this is true. Is it relevant? As long as the Russian people do not control their government, it makes little difference whether they think well of us or ill. It is high time that our leaders stopped treating the Russian people and the Soviet government as one and the same thing. The Russian people, we may safely assume, are basically on our side (whether or not they have the opportunity to listen to American musicians); but their sympathy will not help us win the

Cold War as long as all power is held firmly in the hands of the Communist ruling class.

The exchange program, in Soviet eyes, is simply another operation in Communist political warfare. The people the Kremlin sends over here are, to a man, trained agents of Soviet policy. Some of them are spies, seeking information; all of them are trusted carriers of Communist propaganda. Their mission is not cultural, but political. Their aim is not to inform, but to mislead. Their assignment is not to convey a true image of the Soviet Union, but a false image. The Kremlin's hope is that they will persuade the American people to forget the ugly aspects of Soviet life, and the danger that the Soviet system poses to American freedom.

It is a mistake to measure the success of this Communist operation by the extent to which it converts Americans to Communism. By that test, of course, the operation is almost a complete failure. But the Kremlin's aim is not to make Americans *approve* of Communism, much as they would like that; it is to make us *tolerant* of Communism. The Kremlin knows that our willingness to make sacrifices to halt Communist expansion varies in direct ratio as we are *hostile* to Communism. They know that if Americans regard the Soviet Union as a dangerous, implacable enemy, Communism will not be able to conquer the world. The Communists' purpose, then, is to show that Khrushchev does not have horns,—that he is fundamentally a nice fellow; that the Soviet people are—"ordinary people" just like ourselves; that Communism is just another political system.

It would not have made sense, midway in the Second World War, to promote a Nazi-American exchange program or to invite Hitler to make a state visit to the United States. Unless we cherish victory less today than we did then, we will be equally reluctant to treat Communist agents as friends and welcome guests. The exchange program is a Communist confidence game. Let us not be taken in by it. Let us remember that American confidence in the Soviet government is the very last thing we want.

Many people contend that a "normalization" of Soviet-American relations, as envisaged by the exchange program, is only a logical extension of granting diplomatic recognition to Communists governments. I agree. Accordingly, I think it would be wise for the United States to re-examine the question of its diplomatic relations with Communist regimes. We often hear that recognition permits us to gather information in Communist countries. I am unaware, however, of any advantage that our diplomatic mission in Moscow confers along these lines that does not doubly accrue to the Soviet Union from its diplomatic spy corps in Washington and other American cities. Espionage possibilities aside, I am quite certain that our entire approach to the Cold War would change for the better the moment we announced that the United

States does not regard Mr. Khrushchev's murderous claque as the legitimate rulers of the Russian people or of any other people. Not only would withdrawal of recognition stiffen the American people's attitude toward Communism; it would also give heart to the enslaved peoples and help them to overthrow their captors. Our present policy of not recognizing Red China is eminently right, and the reasons behind that policy apply equally to the Soviet Union and its European satellites. If our objective is to win the Cold War, we will start now by denying our moral support to the very regimes we mean to defeat.

DISARMAMENT For many years, our policy-makers have paid lip-service to the idea of disarmament. This seems to be one of the ways, in modern diplomacy, of proving your virtue. Recently, however—under strong Communist propaganda pressure—we have acted as though we mean this talk to be taken seriously. I cite our government's momentous decision to suspend nuclear tests.

Students of history have always recognized that armament races are a symptom of international friction—not a cause of it. Peace has never been achieved, and it will not in our time, by rival nations suddenly deciding to turn their swords into plowshares. No nation in its right mind will give up the means of defending itself without first making sure that hostile powers are no longer in a position to threaten it.

The Communists leaders are, of course, in their right minds. They would not dream of adopting a policy that would leave them, on balance, relatively weaker than before they adopted such a policy. They might preach general disarmament for propaganda purposes. They also might seriously promote mutual disarmament in certain weapons in the knowledge that their superior strength in other weapons would leave them, on balance, decisively stronger than the West. Thus, in the light of the West's weakness in conventional weapons, it might make sense for the Communists to seek disarmament in the nuclear field; if all nuclear weapons suddenly ceased to exist, much of the world would immediately be laid open to conquest by the masses of Russian and Chinese manpower.

American leaders have not shown a comparable solicitude for our security needs. After the Second World War, the United States had a conventional military establishment rivaling the Soviet Union's, and an absolute monopoly in nuclear power. The former weapon we hastily and irresponsibly dismantled. The latter we failed to exploit politically, and then we proceeded to fritter away our lead by belated entry into the hydrogen bomb and guided missile fields. The result is that we are out-classed in the conventional means for waging land warfare; regarding nuclear weapons, we are approaching the point, if it has not already been reached, where Communist power is equal to our own.

To the impending physical parity in nuclear weapons must be added a psychological factor assiduously cultivated by Communist propaganda. The horrors of all-out warfare are said to be so great that no nation would consider resorting to nuclear weapons unless under direct attack by those same weapons. Now the moment our leaders really accept this, strategic nuclear weapons will be neutralized and Communist armies will be able to launch limited wars without fear of retaliation by our Strategic Air Command. I fear they are coming to accept it, and thus that a military and psychological situation is fast developing in which aggressive Communist forces will be free to maneuver under the umbrella of nuclear terror.

It is in this context that we must view the Communist propaganda drive for a permanent ban on the testing of nuclear weapons, and the inclination of our own leaders to go along with the proposal. There are two preliminary reasons why such proposals ought to be firmly rejected. First, there is no reliable means of preventing the Communists from secretly breaking such an agreement. Our most recent tests demonstrated that underground atomic explosions can be set off without detection. Secondly, we cannot hope to maintain even an effective *strategic* deterrent unless we keep our present nuclear arsenal up to date; this requires testing. But the main point I want to make is that tests are needed to develop *tactical* nuclear weapons for possible use in limited wars. Our military experts have long recognized that for limited warfare purposes we must have a weapons superiority to off-set the Communists' manpower superiority. This means we must develop and perfect a variety of small, clean nuclear weapons; and this in turn means: test-ing. The development of such a weapons system is the only way in which America will be able to fight itself out of the dilemma—one horn of which is superior Communist manpower, the other, the impending neu-tralization of strategic nuclear weapons.

Our government was originally pushed into sus-pending tests by Communist-induced hysteria on the subject of radio-active fallout. However one may rate that danger, it simply has no bearing on the problem at hand. The facts are that there is practically no fall-out from tests conducted above the earth's atmos-phere, and none at all from underground tests. There-fore, the only excuse for suspending tests is that our forbearance somehow contributes to peace. And my answer is that I am unable to see how peace is brought any nearer by a policy that may reduce our relative military strength. Such a policy makes sense only un-der the assumption that Communist leaders have giv-en up their plan for world revolution and will settle for peaceful coexistence—an assumption we make at the risk of losing our national life.

If our objective is victory over Communism, we must achieve superiority in all of the weapons—mili-tary, as well as political and economic—that may be useful in reaching that goal. Such a program costs money, but so long as the money is spent wisely and efficiently, I would spend it. I am not in favor of "economizing" on the nation's safety. As a Conservative, I deplore the huge tax levy that is needed to finance the world's number-one military establishment. But even more do I deplore the prospect of a foreign conquest, which the absence of that establishment would quickly accomplish.

UNITED NATIONS Support of the United Nations, our leaders earnestly proclaim, is one of the cornerstones of American foreign policy. I confess to being more interested in whether American foreign policy has the support of the United Nations.

Here, again, it seems to me that our approach to foreign affairs suffers from a confusion in objectives. Is the perpetuation of an international debating forum, for its own sake, the primary objective of American policy? If so, there is much to be said for our past record of subordinating our national interest to that of the United Nations. If, on the other hand, our primary objective is victory over Communism, we will, as a matter of course, view such organizations as the UN as a possible *means* to that end. Once the question is asked —Does America's participation in the United Nations help or hinder her struggle against world Communism?—it becomes clear that our present commitment to the UN deserves re-examination.

The United Nations, we must remember, is in part

a Communist organization. The Communists always
have at least one seat in its major policy-making body,
the Security Council; and the Soviet Union's permanent veto power in that body allows the Kremlin to
block any action, on a substantial issue, that is contrary to its interests. The Communists also have a size-
able membership in the UN's other policy-making
body, the General Assembly. Moreover, the UN's
working staff, the Secretariat, is manned by hundreds
of Communists agents who are frequently in a position
to sabotage those few UN policies that *are* contrary to
Communist interests. Finally, a great number of non-
Communist United Nations are sympathetic to Soviet
aims—or, at best, are unsympathetic to ours.

We therefore should not be surprised that many
of the policies that emerge from the deliberations of
the United Nations are not policies that are in the best
interest of the United States. United Nations policy is,
necessarily, the product of many different views—
some of them friendly, some of them indifferent to our
interests, some of them mortally hostile. And the result is that our national interests usually suffer when
we subordinate our own policy to the UN's. In nearly
every case in which we have called upon the United
Nations to do our thinking for us, and to make our
policy for us—whether during the Korean War, or in
the Suez crisis, or following the revolution in Iraq—
we have been a less effective foe of Communism than
we otherwise might have been.

Unlike America, the Communists do not respect the UN and do not permit their policies to be affected by it. If the "opinion of mankind," as reflected by a UN resolution, goes against them, they—in effect—tell mankind to go fly a kite. Not so with us; we would rather be approved than succeed, and so are likely to adjust our own views to conform with a United Nations majority. This is not the way to win the Cold War. I repeat: Communism will not be beaten by a policy that is the common denominator of the foreign policies of 80-odd nations, some of which are our enemies, nearly all of which are less determined than we to save the world from Communist domination. Let us, then, have done with submitting major policy decisions to a forum where the opinions of the Sultan of Yeman count equally with ours; where the vote of the United States can be cancelled out by the likes of "Byelorussia."

I am troubled by several other aspects of our UN commitment. First—and here again our Cold War interests are dan.aged—the United Nations provides a unique forum for Communist propaganda. We too, of course, can voice our views at the UN; but the Communists' special advantage is that their lies and misrepresentations are elevated to the level of serious international debate. By recognizing the right of Communist regimes to participate in the UN as equals, and by officially acknowledging them as "peace-loving," we grant Communist propaganda a presumption of reasonableness and plausibility it otherwise would not have.

Second, the UN places an unwarranted financial burden on the American taxpayer. The Marxist formula, "from each according to his ability . . ."—under which contributions to the UN and its specialized agencies are determined—does not tally with the American concept of justice. The United States is currently defraying roughly a third of all United Nations expenses. That assessment should be drastically reduced. The UN should not operate as a charity. Assessments should take into account the benefits received by the contributor-nation.

Finally, I fear that our involvement in the United Nations may be leading to an unconstitutional surrender of American sovereignty. Many UN activities have already made strong inroads against the sovereign powers of Member Nations. This is neither the time nor place to discuss the merits of yielding sovereign American rights—other than to record my unequivocal opposition to the idea. It is both the time and place, however, to insist that any such discussion take place within the framework of a proposed constitutional amendment—and not, clandestinely, in the headquarters of some UN agency.

Withdrawal from the United Nations is probably not the answer to these problems. For a number of reasons that course is unfeasible. We should make sure, however, that the nature of our commitment is such as to advance American interests; and that will involve changes in some of our present attitudes and policies toward the UN. Let the UN firsters—of whom there are many in this country—put their enthusiasm for "international cooperation" in proper perspective. Let them understand that victory over Communism must come *before* the achievement of lasting peace. Let them, in a word, keep their eyes on the target.

AID TO COMMUNIST GOVERNMENTS There is one aspect of our policy that *is* offensive-minded — in the minds of its authors, anyway. Its effect, unfortunately, is exactly opposite to the one intended.

Some time ago our leaders advanced the theory that Communist satellite regimes would, with our help, gradually break their ties with the Soviet Union and "evolve" political systems more in keeping with our notions of freedom and justice. Accordingly, America adopted the policy of giving aid to Communist governments whose relations with Moscow seemed to be strained. And that policy gave birth to a slogan: "America seeks the liberation of enslaved peoples— not by revolution—but through evolution." Under the aegis of this slogan, we are sending hundreds of millions of dollars to the Communist government of Poland, having already given more than a billion dollars to the Communist government of Yugoslavia.

In my view, this money has not only been wasted; it has positively promoted the Communist cause. It has *not* made Communist governments less Communist. It has *not* caused Communist governments to change sides in the Cold War. It *has* made it easier for Communist governments to keep their subjects enslaved. And none of these results should have come as a surprise.

One does not have to take the view that a Communist regime will never "evolve" into a non-Communist one (though I tend to it) in order to see that this is practically impossible as long as the Soviet Union possesses the military and political power to prevent it. The Kremlin may, for its own purposes, permit certain "liberalization" tendencies in satellite countries; it may even permit small deviations from the approved Soviet foreign policy line. It will do so sometimes to confuse the West, sometimes as a prudent means of relieving internal pressures. But it will never let things go too far. Hungary proved that. The moment a Communist government threatens to become a non-Communist one, or threatens to align itself with the West against the Soviet Union, the Kremlin will take steps to bring the defecting government into line.

Hungary proved this truth, and Poland has proved that dissident Communists learned it. Western leaders, unfortunately, were much less perceptive. In the Fall of 1956, there appeared to be a breach between Gomulka's government and the Kremlin. Many Westerners joyfully proclaimed that Poland was pulling away from Communism, and hoping to hasten this movement, our government began to send the Gomul-

ka regime American aid. The succeeding years witnessed two facts: 1. Our money made it easier for Gomulka's regime to deal with its economic problems; 2.
Gomulka moved into an even closer relationship with
the Soviet government. Gomulka knew, as American
policy-makers ought to have known, that the price of
abandoning Communism is a Budapest-type blood
bath. This, of course, need not be the case were America prepared to come to the aid of people who want to
strike out for freedom. But as long as we give Soviet
military forces a free hand in Eastern Europe, it is the
height of folly to try to bribe Communist governments
into becoming our friends.

We must realize that the captive *peoples* are our
friends and potential allies—not their rulers. A truly
offensive-minded strategy would recognize that the
captive peoples are our strongest weapon in the war
against Communism, and would encourage them to
overthrow their captors. A policy of strengthening
their captors can only postpone that upheaval within
the Communist Empire that is our best hope of defeating Communism without resorting to nuclear war.

**TOWARD
VICTORY**   By measuring each aspect of our foreign
policy against the standard—Is it helpful
in defeating the enemy?—we can understand why the past fourteen years have been marked
by frustration and failure. We have not gotten ahead
because we have been travelling the wrong road.

It is less easy to stake out the right road. For in terms of our own experience it is a new road we seek, and one therefore that will hold challenges and perils that are different (though hardly graver) from those with which we are now familiar. Actually, the "new" road is as old as human history: it is the one that successful political and military leaders, having arrived at a dispassionate "estimate of the situation," always follow when they are in a war they mean to win. From our own estimate of the situation, we know the *direction* we must take; and our standard—Is it helpful in defeating Communism?—will provide guideposts all along the way. There are some that can be observed even now:

1. The key guidepost is the Objective, and we must never lose sight of it. It is not to wage a struggle against Communism, but to win it.

OUR GOAL MUST BE VICTORY 2. Our strategy must be primarily offensive in nature. Given the dynamic, revolutionary character of the enemy's challenge, we cannot win merely by trying to hold our own. In addition to paring his blows, we must strike our own. In addition to guarding our frontiers, we must try to puncture his. In addition to keeping the free world free, we must try to make the Communist world free. To these ends, we must always try to engage the enemy at times and places, and with weapons, of our own choosing.

3. We must strive to achieve and maintain military superiority. Mere parity will not do. Since we can never match the Communists in manpower, our equipment and weapons must more than offset his advantage in numbers. We must also develop a limited war capacity. For this latter purpose, we should make every effort to achieve decisive superiority in small, clean nuclear weapons.

4. We must make America economically strong. We have already seen why economic energy must be released from government strangulation if individual freedom is to survive. Economic emancipation is equally imperative if the nation is to survive. America's maximum economic power will be forged, not under bureaucratic direction, but in freedom.

5. In all of our dealings with foreign nations, we must behave like a great power. Our national posture must reflect strength and confidence and purpose, as well as good will. We need not be bellicose, but neither should we encourage others to believe that American rights can be violated with impunity. We must protect American nationals and American property and American honor—everywhere. We may not make foreign peoples love us—no nation has ever succeeded in that —but we can make *them respect us*. And *respect* is the stuff of which enduring friendships and firm alliances are made.

6. We should adopt a discriminating foreign aid pol-

icy. American aid should be furnished only to friendly, anti-Communist nations that are willing to join with us in the struggle for freedom. Moreover, our aid should take the form of loans or technical assistance, not gifts. And we should insist, moreover, that such nations contribute their fair share to the common cause.

7. We should declare the world Communist movement an outlaw in the community of civilized nations. Accordingly, we should withdraw diplomatic recognition from all Communist governments including that of the Soviet Union, thereby serving notice on the world that we regard such governments as neither legitimate nor permanent.

8. We should encourage the captive peoples to revolt against their Communist rulers. This policy must be pursued with caution and prudence, as well as courage. For while our enslaved friends must be told we are anxious to help them, we should discourage premature uprisings that have no chance of success. The freedom fighters must understand that the time and place and method of such uprisings will be dictated by the needs of an overall world strategy. To this end we should establish close liaison with underground leaders behind the Iron Curtain, furnishing them with printing presses, radios, weapons, instructors: the paraphernalia of a full-fledged Resistance.

9. We should encourage friendly peoples that have

the means and desire to do so to undertake offensive
operations for the recovery of their homelands. For
example, should a revolt occur inside Red China, we
should encourage and support guerrilla operations on
the mainland by the Free Chinese. Should the situation develop favorably, we should encourage the South
Koreans and the South Vietnamese to join Free Chinese forces in a combined effort to liberate the enslaved peoples of Asia.

10. We must—ourselves—be prepared to undertake
military operations against vulnerable Communist regimes. Assume we have developed nuclear weapons
that can be used in land warfare, and that we have
equipped our European divisions accordingly. Assume
also a major uprising in Eastern Europe, such as occurred in Budapest in 1956. In such a situation, we
ought to present the Kremlin with an ultimatum for-
bidding Soviet intervention, and be prepared, if the
ultimatum is rejected, to move a highly mobile task
force equipped with appropriate nuclear weapons to
the scene of the revolt. Our objective would be to con-
front the Soviet Union with superior force in the immediate vicinity of the uprising and to compel a Soviet withdrawal. An actual clash between American
and Soviet armies would be unlikely; the mere threat
of American action, coupled with the Kremlin's
knowledge that the fighting would occur amid a hostile population and could easily spread to other areas,
would probably result in Soviet acceptance of the ultimatum. The Kremlin would also be put on notice, of

course, that resort to long-range bombers and missiles would prompt automatic retaliation in kind. On this level, we would invite the Communist leaders to choose between total destruction of the Soviet Union, and accepting a local defeat . . . Had we the will and the means for it in 1956, such a policy would have saved the Hungarian Revolution.

This is hard counsel. But it is hard, I think, not for what it says, but for saying it openly. Such a policy involves the risk of war? Of course; but any policy, short of surrender, does that. Any policy that successfully frustrates the Communists' aim of world domination runs the risk that the Kremlin will choose to lose in a kamikaze-finish. It is hard counsel because it frankly acknowledges that war may be the price of freedom, and thus intrudes on our national complacency. But is it really so hard when it goes on to search for the most likely means of safeguarding both our lives *and* our freedom? Is it so hard when we think of the risks that were taken to create our country?—risks on which our ancestors openly and proudly staked their "lives, fortunes, and sacred honor." Will we do less to *save* our country?

The risks I speak of are risks on our terms, instead of on Communist terms. *We*, not they, would select the time and place for a test of wills. *We*, not they, would have the opportunity to bring maximum strength to bear on that test. *They*, not we, would have to decide between fighting for limited objectives under unfavorable circumstances, or backing down. And these are immense advantages.

The future, as I see it, will unfold along one of two paths. Either the Communists will retain the offensive; will lay down one challenge after another; will invite us in local crisis after local crisis to choose between all-out war and limited retreat; and will force us, ultimately, to surrender or accept war under the most disadvantageous circumstances. Or *we* will summon the will and the means for taking the initiative, and wage a war of attrition against them—and hope, thereby, to bring about the internal disintegration of the Communist empire. One course runs the risk of war, and leads, in any case, to probable defeat. The other runs the risk of war, and holds forth the promise of victory. For Americans who cherish their lives, but their freedom more, the choice cannot be difficult.